I0002364

GETTING START WITH ESP32 AND ARDUINO

IoT Device Projects, LED Matrix, ESP32 Cam Module IOT Practical Approach and more

By

Janani Sathish

Table of Contents

GETTING TO KNOW YOUR ESP3

Getting to know your ESP32 In this project, we will learn the following What is ESP32? The features of ESP32 and how it compares to the wildly popular ESP8266. So lets dive right into the world of the ESP32. The ESP32 is a SOC or system on chip microcontroller.

It is manufactured by Espressif, a Shanghai-based company with an expertise in Low Power IOT solutions . It was introduced at the end of 2016.

The ESP32 can be called as the successor to the IOT enthusiasts favorite the

ESP8266. It is specifically designed for low power IOT or the Internet of Things applications.

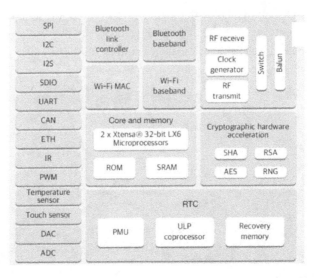

So what makes the ESP32 stand out? Lets take a closer look at its primary features and how the ESP32 compares to the ESP8266 Let us look at the CPO first the ESB 32 contains two low power dense silica extends out 32 bit microprocessors. Lets look at the CPU first. The ESP32 contains two low power Tensilica Xtensa 32-bit microprocessors This is an upgrade over its predecessor, the ESP8266, which just had a single core Tensilica Xtensa 32-bit microprocessor. The ESP32 is clocked at a faster 160 MHz CPU and can be clocked up to a maximum of 240 MHz. 160 MHz CPU and can be clocked up to a maximum of 240 MHz. All of this means overall better performance and faster computation. The ESP32 has faster Wi-Fi built right into it when compared to the ESP8266. This is a huge deal because this allows the ESP32 based development boards to be truly wireless, , unlike traditional microcontroller boards like the Arduino. The ESP32 implements full TCP/IP, b/g/n/e/i WLAN MAC protocol.

It can connect to most Wi-Fi routers with ease which makes it highly compatible to use. The ESP32 also overcomes what the ESP8266 lacked, inbuilt Bluetooth. Which means integrating it as a standalone unit with Bluetooth. enabled devices like your smartphone is now possible. The ESP32 has dual Bluetooth support, for both Bluetooth version 4. 2 or Bluetooth classic and Bluetooth Bluetooth low energy or Bluetooth Smart. This makes it ideal for low power applications like wearables, health-based sensors, beacons etc. It also has built-in sensors like the Hall Effect sensor and temperature sensor. It even has touch sensitive gpio pins! This makes the ESP32 self-contained without the need for interfacing separate sensors for measuring magnetic fields or temperature . In comparison, the ESP8266 does not have any of these sensors built into it. The ESP32 has support for peripheral interfaces like SPI I2C, I2S, CAN and UART.

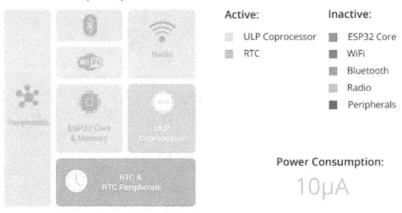

This allows the ESP32 to interface easily with an extensive range of sensors and actuators which communicate via these protocols One of the more attractive features of the ESP32 is the Deep Sleep mode, which when activated consumes only about 0. 15 uA to 10uA of current. To put this in perspective, in the normal mode, the ESP32 consumes 240 mA of current, a staggering 24000 times the deep sleep mode current! This translates to your power hungry projects lasting years on battery power! The ESP32 is powered by 40nm technology, making it highly robust and helping it to satisfy the demands for efficient power usage, security, reliability, and high performance.

The ESP32 is jam-packed with features which the ESP8266 lacked It is apparent now that the ESP32 has a significant advantage over the ESP8266 in all aspects All of these features combined make the ESP32 an ideal standalone microcontroller for your mobile wearable and Internet of Things projects. We recommend you to go through the ESP32s datasheet in the resources section to understand the power requirements and the absolute maximum power ratings It would also help you to further explore features in depth before getting your hands dirty with the actual hardware. In this project, we learned about what ESP32 is, the features of ESP32 and how it compares to the ESP8266 In the next project you will learn about the Sparkfun ESP32 Thing development board.

EXPLORING THE SPARKFUN ESP32 THING

Exploring the Sparkfun ESP32 Thing In this project , we will take a look at. The Sparkfun ESP32 Thing development board and its onboard featuresIn the previous project. , we took a look at the ESP32 microcontroller chip and how it compares to the ESP8266.

You may have already got a glimpse of the plethora of capabilities that the ESP32 has to offer. The ESP32 in itself is pretty non-intuitive when it comes to using it for development purposes and can be quite a challenge to use. Here comes the Sparkfun ESP32 Thing to the rescue! Coming in at just under 22 dollars , the Sparkfun ESP32 thing is a tiny, cheap yet a powerful development board based on the ESP32 microcontroller chip The Sparkfun ESP32 Thing takes the humble ESP32 chip and converts it into a development powerhouse So lets take a quick tour of the board. . . First, you will find the MicroUSB type B connector . It is used to power up the board as well as program itIts recommended that you power the board via your computers standard USB port which supplies 5V using a USB to MicroUSB cable. The Thing has an onboard 3. 3V voltage regulator so you can supply voltage greater than 3. 3V. point three volts next to the micro USP connector is a two pin GST connector for powering the board Next to the MicroUSB connector is the 2-Pin JST connector for powering the board via a single-cell LiPO batteryYou can use either of these two to power up the board So what happens when you try to power the board via both the LiPO as well as the MicroUSB connector? The onboard charging circuitry on the thing takes over.

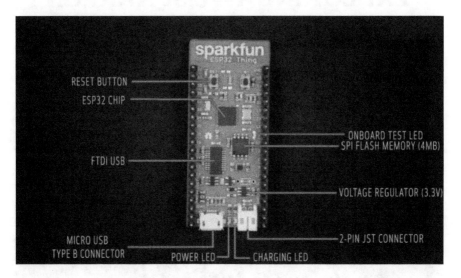

It starts charging the LiPO battery! Cool isn't it. This is the ESP32 chip itself This is the 4Mb SPI flash memory Here we have the FTDI USB to serial converter chip This is the ESB to reduce poverty which lets you know if the ESB 32 is powered on next to that we have the ESP32s charging led, which lets you know if the LiPO battery is charging. This is the onboard test LED, which can be accessed as PIN 5 This will come in handy at later stages in this project This is the RESET button which lets you to hard reset the board. This is the onboard push button which can be accessed as PIN 0 The Sparkfun ESP32 thing breaks out the ESP32 chips pins into two breadboard compatible rows.

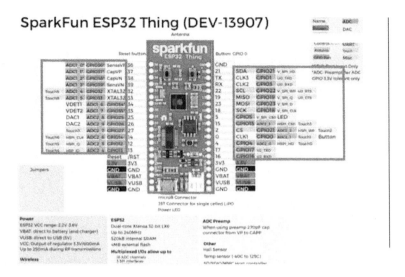

The board has multiplexed I/Os. There are 28 GPIO pins,18 ADC channels, 3 SPI interfaces, 3 UART interfaces , 2 I2C interfaces, 2 I2S interfaces, 16 LED PWM outputs, 2 DACs and 10 capacitive touch inputs These are the default pins for I2C, I2S and PWM. The other I2C, I2S and PWM interfaces can be configured to any of the GPIOs except pins 34 to 39, which are input only. Pin multiplexing allows the same set of pins to be used for multiple purposes. This helps you to choose which pin should be for SPI, UART, I2C, etc. This also allows the size of the board to be small, as the number of pins becomes lesser compared to if each pin had separate functionality Now let's talk about the power pins. The onboard voltage regulator on the ESP32 thing can reliably supply current up to 600 mA. For most IOT projects this much current would suffice. While using Wi-Fi, however, the current draw can be as high as 250 mA. Thus the total current which your peripheral your peripheral devices attached to the board can draw should be less than 350 mA. The output of the regulator is broken out to the sides of the board .

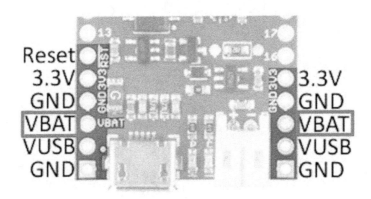

There are two 3. 3 volt pins, which can be used to power up sensors and actuators running on 3. 3V. Next we have 2 VBAT pins, which essentially allows you to power up the board from a LiPO battery which does not have a JST connector. Then we have 2 VUSB which can be used to power up the board via an external power supply like a battery with a maximum safe voltage of 6V. An important thing to note the I/O pins on the ESP32 are not 5V tolerant. Connecting 5V peripherals to the thing would require you to level shift to 3. 3V Remember, do not try to connect power supplies which lie outside the safe range of operation , as this can destroy the internal components in the board and cause permanent damage. Finally, at the end of the board. , we have the PCB trace antenna for the Wi-Fi. This completes the tour of the Sparkfun ESP32 thing development board. In this project, we took a tour of the Sparkfun ESP32 thing development board and looked at its key features. In the next project, you will learn about the Sparkfun ESP32 Thing development board

HOOKING UP THE SPARKFUN ESP32 THING TO THE ARDUINO IDE

, hooking up the Sparkfun ESP32 Thing to the Arduino IDE In this project we will learn the following Installing the ESP32 core on the Arduino IDE Blinking an onboard LED on the Thing There are many ways of programming the Thing, but one of the easiest and most intuitive ways of programming the Thing is through the Arduino IDE. You can download the latest version of the Arduino IDE for both Mac and Windows from the link provided in the resources section.

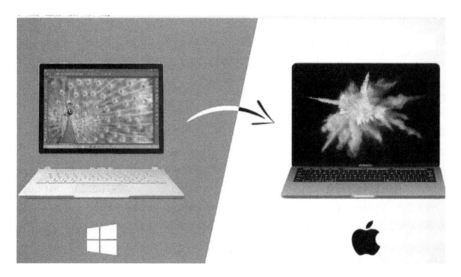

Everything explained from now onwards onwards will apply to both Windows and Mac unless explicitly stated. After installing the Arduino IDE , open it and you will have the development environment itself Firstly, you need to go to the tools section wherein you will find the boards section. If you select the Arduino Boards Manager option, you will see a list of the boards which come preinstalled. From Arduino version 1. 6. 2 all Arduino AVR boards are preinstalled. But for other microcontrollers like the ESP32, you would need to install additional cores. The Arduino boards manager makes it really convenient to install the Arduino core for the ESP32 Now if you search our particular board which is the ESP32, you will not find it. Thats because we need to install a third party core for the ESP32. To do this, go to file and then preferences In Mac you can find this option if you go to Arduino and then preferences. You will find a field called as the Additional

Board Manager URLs. The field needs a specific type of file This is a file written in JSON format which needs to entered in the field for the additional boards manager to fetch the list of third party cores Dont worry, you can find the link in the resources section Copy the link and paste it into the field.

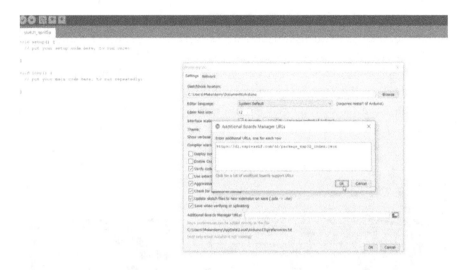

The additional boards manager will fetch the ESP32 cores developed by espressif systems. Now click here and paste the link. Now you can click on ok to exit the preferences window. Now if you go to the Boards Manager, and search for ESP32, you will find the list of boards. Here we can see that the package includes the ESP32 development module, which has the Arduino core for the ESP32. This will help us make the ESP32 compatible with the Arduino for using Arduino libraries and source code. You can download any release you want, but you would want to download the latest version as it contains updates and fixes previous bugs. To check all the releases for the Arduino ESP32 core, you can find the link to the Githubs espressif repository for the ESP32 in the resources section. We will be using Version 1. 0. 1 as of this date throughout the project. Now install and wait for it to download and install the packages Once installed, close the board managers window. Now if you go to tools and check scroll down to check for the boards, you will find the ESP32 dev module. Now you are all set to program the Thing. This is the Arduino development environment. Arduino makes it really easy to write code It does most of the work for you The arduino language is nothing but a set of C/C++ functions which gets called everytime you run the program In Arduino , the program you run is called a Sketch This is what gets uploaded to the microcontroller board. First things first, lets look at these two functions over here Why are they here in the first place These are functions which get called whenever you compile and run an Arduino Sketch The first one is the Setup function The Void here is used to specify that the function itself does not return any value The setup function is used to initialize variables, libraries, declare pin modes etc. This runs only once in the program. Now coming to the Loop function here this is where you write your actual code This will run multiple times. Lets look at an example to blink the onboard LED on the thing to get a better idea. First, connect your Thing via the USB to MicroUSB cable cable to any of your computers USB port to start programming. You need to select the correct serial communication port also referred to as the COM port in arduino. You can find this under tool and port. For Mac users , the file which maps to this port is the usb serial port. Since the Sparkfun ESP32 thing has an FTDI USB to TTL Serial converter built in , you dont need to use an external one to program it. This makes it super convenient to program it Once you have selected your serial port, you can upload a blank sketch to test if your code is compiling and uploading correctly. To do this just select upload. Here you will find your debug messages after uploading your code. You will also get information on the amount of memory your whole code and variables are consuming. Hence optimizing your code is essential when your microcontroller has limited memory. If you have successfully uploaded your code to the ESP32, you will get this message Now lets go back to the code to blink the on-board LED on the Thing.

File Edit Sketch Tools Help

```
LED_Blink

int led = 5;

void setup() {
  // initialize digital pin led as an output.
  pinMode(led, OUTPUT);
}

// the loop function runs over and over again forever
void loop() {
  digitalWrite(led, HIGH);   // turn the LED on (HIGH is the voltage level)
  delay(1000);               // wait for a second
  digitalWrite(led, LOW);    // turn the LED off by making the voltage LOW
  delay(1000);               // wait for a second
}
```

The LED on the Thing can be accessed as Pin number 5 in arduino Here we are first assigning a variable LED as integer number 5. Now this variable LED can be accessed as Pin 5 on the Arduino Here we are setting the particular pin number 5 as the output. We need to do this only once, hence we include this in the setup

15

function Here the digital Write sets the particular pin, in our case Pin no 5 as High or Low The delay of 1000 is in milliseconds which means toggling the LED on and off every 1 second. Now upload the sketch You will be asked to save the file first . Once uploaded, you will see the onboard LED on the thing blinking.

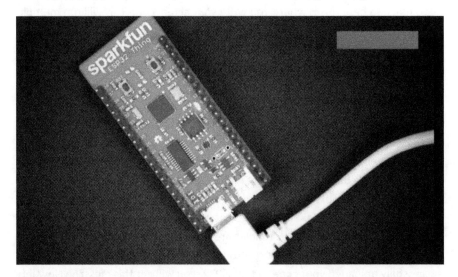

The onboard LED on the Thing can be used as a test LED to debug certain errors in the code. The onboard button can be accessed as PIN 0 in a similar way . It is also a nice feature if you dont want to use an external button for testing purposes. In this project, we learned how to install the ESP32 core on the Arduino IDE and blinking an onboard LED on the thing. In the next project you will learn to read the onboard sensor values on the thing.

WORKING WITH THE ON BOARD SENSORS ON THE THING

Working with the On Board Sensors on the Thing In this project we will learn the following How the temperature sensor on the Thing works and reading its Values How the Hall Effect sensor on the Thing works and reading its Values. How the Touch sensitive GPIOs on the Thing works and reading its Values.

Lets now look at the onboard sensors on the Sparkfun ESP32 Thing. As you have seen in the previous projects, the ESP32 microcontroller chip on the Thing has a temperature sensor, a Hall Effect sensor and Touch sensitive GPIOs built right into it. The onboard temperature sensor on the Thing is different from your usual temperature sensors. Instead of measuring the ambient temperature, the sensor measures the internal temperature of the ESP32 microcontroller chip itself. The temperature sensor has a range of -40 degree Celsius to 125 degrees Celsius. However, the absolute temperature measurements are not accurate This is because an offset temperature gets introduced with a different value for each ESP32 chip manufactured. So you may ask, then why even have a temperature sensor inside a chip that is not accurate and does not measure ambient temperature? Well, the temperature sensor on the Thing is not meant for that in the first place. The sensor is useful if you want to measure temperature difference in your chip, and not the absolute value. To illustrate this lets look at an Arduino code to measure the onboard temperature sensors value when it is connected to the Wi-Fi. We will learn about connecting to the Wi-Fi in detail in the next section. You can find the code in the Resources Section. This part of the code is used to inform the C++ compiler in arduino to compile the C functions/libraries along with the C++ libraries as one module Next we have the Serial. begin function, which is used to set the Baud rate for serial transmission between your computer and the Thing.

In Arduino the baud rate is the same as the bit rate That means 1 baud = 1 bit Next, we have the Serial. print function, which prints the data to serial port in ASCII format. This function is used to get the raw temperature values in Fahrenheit. This is converted to Celsius by using the following formula. The delay here is introduced to run the code continuously at intervals of 1 second. Now you can compile and upload the code. Once uploaded you can go to tools and select Serial Monitor.

The Serial Monitor is a tool which allows you to send commands from your computer to the Thing. It also helps in reading the incoming Serial data from the Thing and to display it. Now select the correct baud rate which we have set in the Serial. begin function. As you can see, you are getting the temperature readings in Celsius So now how do you actually make sense out of it? The temperature sensor readings can be helpful to determine any abnormal changes in internal temperature of the chip. This can happen in case there is an inherent malfunction in the chip itself which can cause the chip to become hot. In which case measuring the temperature difference would be useful Now lets look at how to use the inbuilt Hall Effect sensor on the ESP32. The Hall Effect sensor is used to determine the direction and strength of a magnetic field It can be used for proximity sensing applications. This is the code to measure the Hall Effect sensor readings Here we are setting the baud rate as 115200 The higher the baud rate, faster is the transmission. The Hall Effect sensor produces a changing voltage with varying magnetic field This voltage is measured by the internal Analog to Digital converter. Hall read is an inbuilt function to read the Analog to Digital converter values This is stored in a local variable called measurement. This is then printed out to the Serial port. Now we will use another tool, not the serial monitor this time. This tool is the Serial Plotter. The Serial plotter is a great way to visualize your incoming serial data You can go to tools and then select the Serial plotter You can also open the Serial Monitor to view the readings in text. In the Serial Plotter you can see that the readings are noisy.

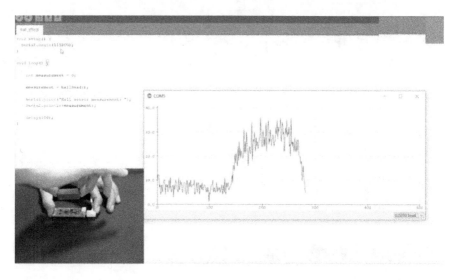

Lets see what happens when we bring a magnet close to the ESP32 chip on the Thing. The value suddenly shoot up. Now if we turn over the magnet, you will see that values drop down in the negative direction Hence the Hall Effect sensor is able to measure the direction of the Magnetic field. If you vary the magnets. distance from the chip, you will see that the readings will vary according to the distance Hence the Hall Effect sensor in the Thing can also measure strength of the magnetic field. Now lets look at the touch sensitive GPIOs on the Thing. We can choose from any of the ten touch sensitive GPIO Pins . Here we are choosing GPIO pin number 15. The touchRead function is used to read the analog to digital converted values and print it to the Serial monitor and Serial plotter.

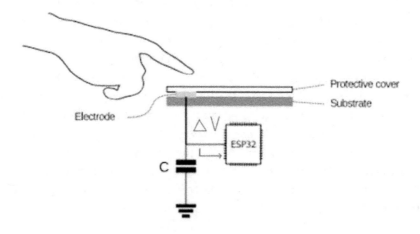

The Touch sensitive GPIOs on the Thing work on the concept of capacitive sensing. It changes capacitance based on the distance of your finger from the GPIO pin This change in capacitance is converted to voltage change and measured by the ADC on the Thing. Now if we open the Serial monitor, we can see the change in analog values when we touch the pin. In this Project, we learned how the temperature sensor, Hall Effect Sensor, and touch sensitive GPIOs work and reading Values from the same In this section we cover the following introduction to the project getting to know you. Yes P3 do exploring this park for an ESB terrible thing looking up this park fan yes Peter relating to the Arduino I. D. working with the onboard sensors on the thing in the next section you will learn about connecting to the Thing wirelessly.

WEB DASHBOARD

We're gonna create an Web Dashboard on un-free to use IoT program and also create the proper sketch so that you can control here an LED or from the Internet in real-time.

Also can manipulate the brightness level of the LED. And we are sending real-time sensor data from our Arduino to the web dashboard and visualize it afterwards. We're also add some optimizations that went on. Thresholds will be reached. Then we get the notification on our smartphone. We're developing the Arduino code step-by-step, and all codes are available for downloads.

FREE IOT BROKERS

Let's start with some quick over you. Blink is one of the IoT protocols, which I think is really, really handy because they have a good library. And also we can start right away. The next cool thing is they have a free account. That means we can connect two devices. Five uses maximum basic widgets, but it's enough for us.

And also we have one week of historical data. Bus pricing sources is by $5 each month and have ten devices. It's awesome. Reasonable price when you want to add more devices to you. Blinker count. But there are also other IoT protocols which I can recommend. And F If you have steam one setup, there were all in the same way. For example, thing i o, It's also nice platform where you can connect with you ESPs and make some nice IoT devices. Thing i o is more in the mCPU and Tege a environment. It's not so straightforward, but also easy to use when you like MQTT. And I also can recommend these because all of these platforms has been having free account. And this is in my opinion, always a good way to make the first experience and afterwards. You can also choose if you want to go pro or not.

WIRING

Let us jump right into the wiring part. I have fear, an ESP 32and temperature sensor.

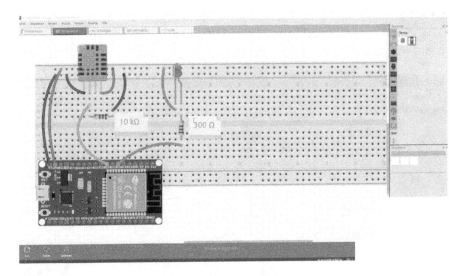

The 112 resistors with 300ohms and ten kilo ohms, one LED, and a few jumper cables. In general, here I have connection to five worlds to ground the four pins of the VHD L11. The first one is connected to the VCC, him to five-year-old, for example. The second one is the data line. We are connecting the data line. For example, GPIO. Twenty-five, GPIO means general purpose input and output for our ESP 32. And also there is recommended and ten kilo-ohm resistor going from the data line to their BCC. It's pull up resistors that we have in good sign on our data line. The certs pin is not connected and default pin of the DHT alignment goes to grants. Then on the GPIOs 32 I think is that we're going to the resistor. The resistor output in our LED him to the anode and the blood side and the cathode or the minus side that goes to ground. That's on what we have here. So the main purpose of this sketch, or if this warren part would be that we sent the data of temperature, humidity date down to our blink website. And also that we can manipulate and switching on and off the LED via the web dashboards. So let's focus on the varying part here. So I feel the components. And now the USBE certainly tool I have here, the developer port. I think in a second, can you also can use an

ESPN 8266, but then be awhile you have to implement other libraries. First of all, I make the connection. Similarly a bit in. Make the connection from five volt pin to glass on the breadboard. And also with the grounds. Also I recommend to look at you are pinouts because I have fear. The second pin, knot and ground It's a cmd pin.

But I saw an add-on pin outs from the ESP sorted to the second opinions grounds, my ground pennies here. So let's check your pin outs according to your ESPN so that you have the proper and right pins. This is our ADHD 11 project will also work with ADHD 22. This one has not so much accuracy, but for our project It's totally fine. Sticking.

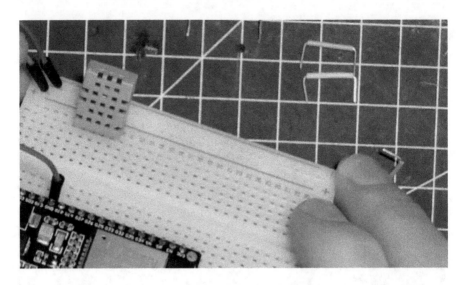

Dan. Fear some short circuits for making the connection. Then we're going to get the first pin two plus. We have also the last pin, two minus or the ground pin. The second goes the data pin. The data bim goes to Let me see, Twenty-five. Twenty-five is here. And also we have ten kilo ohm resistor. Ten kilo ohm resistor goes toVcc and that's disconnection. Then once again, the output sir 72 or think goes to the resistor and the resistance jumps over to the next part of the breadboard. And then I have feared the LED and steady long opinion would be the plus poem. Smaller than d plus, minus. We're connecting the minus side. So the ground off debt bradyzoites, That's our finished circuits. So once again, connects plus and ground from the ESP into the breadboard.

The first pin will be the blast. The second data pin is not connected off the DHT E11. The last one is two, goes to the ground. Also add ten kilo pull-up resistor to the data pin. Pin goes to G 25 and the LED goes from GPIO. 32. Resistors reentered ohms, the LED. That's what we want now. Short little circuits for our IoT device.

DATASTREAMS

We are now back at our blink website and I'm assuming that you have already registered, you set up an accountant logged in. And it then you should see the same website, nearly the same websites I have here. Let's jump right into the templates. It should be on the left side. And I already have one template here, but we are going to the right top corner and creating a new template.

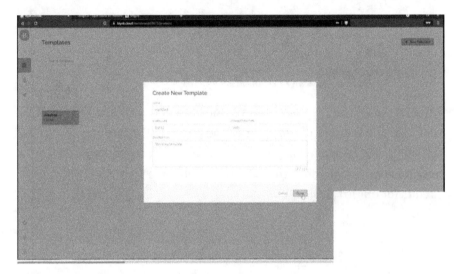

We're typing here in the name as you would like. Here, we have two options. The hardware under connection type, I always are only use wife team so far, and it's a hardware you can choose here, your microcontroller, for example, ESPN thirty two, eighty two, sixty six or also at respiratory buyer can add a description and then you hit done. Now we have our main template.

And with this template we can organize ourselves also the virtual pins and the web dashboard. And this is what we do know. We have a felt their configuration and disinformation. We get a little bit later so you can copy it, but you don't have to. We are jumping now into data streams. The data streams are the connection from the dashboard to our ESP, where now connecting virtual pins here on the dashboard and later on in the sketch so that we can hear fear and data exchange. The main purpose will be in this project that we switch on the LED and also within slider changed uprightness.

29

Therefore, we need two data streams, virtual pin. The first one will be brightness. I select virtual pin one. We are only taking into churn this example and we say 0 to 100, sera means completely dark and 100 different brightness can also define them default value. If you want to. Under advanced, I would like to turn on switch with latest.

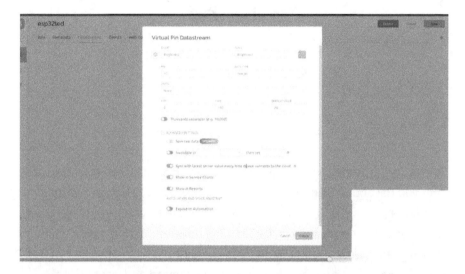

So we're really every time device connected to the Cloud. That's really convenient. So you always get the last state of your LED. Then click on Create. We're making new DataStream because we also wanted to switch on and off the LED. Therefore, we are defining LED, making an wheat, for example, integer min, max one because we only need two states. And I also want to define sync with latest. And the default value will always be theorems or it should be off. Dan, click on Create. Let's all what we need so far. Then. Don't forget to click here on safe. And now we have already insert our two data streams which will be later connected in our sketch for the data exchange.

WEB DASHBOARD

As a next step, we set up our web dashboard here on the menu, and we'll click on Edit. And T, We have a few widgets. Not all are available forus because it's in the basic version. We only have fewer and slider, for example, drag and drop it here into our dashboard and also and switch.

The main idea is that we set up now and the communication from the web dashboards to the ESP. And later on we're also sending data from the ESP and visualize it on a dashboard. But this will be the first step. So Trek and dropped the elements here on the dashboard. And when you hover on the widget, there's a gear symbol.

Then you click on the stream, we're selecting brightness were already have defined here. Everything click and save. The switch. Choose source, LED. We too safe. Don't forget to save on the whole dashboards. And that's all for making a template for the VAP dashboards.

ADD A DEVICE

So now it's on the time that we are making the next step. So we're clicking on search or under main page.

And we want to add here and device on the right top corner, clicking a new device, Dan, we're selecting from templates. Choose template. We are sent drop-down menu, click on it, select USP to LED.

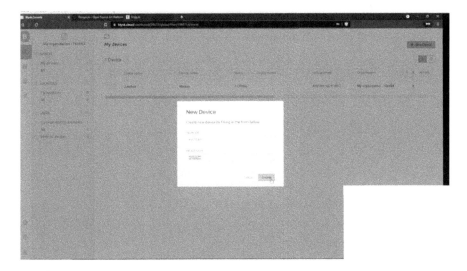

Device name already inserts, and then click on Create. Here we have our secret source because this is what we need afterwards forth USB connection. Now I can show you here are the dashboard which were already implemented in the template. And this is nowhere afterwards we can make some changes.

But as you can see, my device is not online. That's because we haven't got implemented it. So we are created in template and device. And in the next project, we're gonna set up this sketch.

LIBRARIES AND COMPATIBILITY

Before we start with decoding part, I would like to introduce you to the main library of blink. I give you the link also. It's attached in the sketch by itself. But what I would like to focus here is we have fear examples. Now we can choose, for example, board swiping.

Here you have a lot of examples for node MCU, for ESP 8266stand-alone, it's at. And I'm using the ESP 32 WiFi example. With this sketch by itself, you should make and connection to the blinks out, which we do later on. But just go through the main basic steps. So we have here and define a serial.

```
24
25    Please be sure to select the right ESP32 module
26    in the Tools -> Board menu!
27
28    Change WiFi ssid, pass, and Blynk auth token to run :)
29    Feel free to apply it to any other example. It's simple!
30    *************************************************************/
31
32    /* Comment this out to disable prints and save space */
33    #define BLYNK_PRINT Serial
34
35    /* Fill-in your Template ID (only if using Blynk Cloud) */
36    //#define BLYNK_TEMPLATE_ID   "YourTemplateID"
37
38
39    #include <WiFi.h>
40    #include <WiFiClient.h>
41    #include <BlynkSimpleEsp32.h>
42        *
43    // You should get Auth Token in the Blynk App.
44    // Go to the Project Settings (nut icon).
45    char auth[] = "YourAuthToken";
46
47    // Your WiFi credentials.
48    // Set password to "" for open networks.
49    char ssid[] = "YourNetworkName";
50    char pass[] = "YourPassword";
```

We may can, we feel we have to include three libraries, Wi-Fi, wi-fi client and the blink simply ESP certainty to them which already included one you have included are in starts the whole Blink library. And then we have to define three variables. The char for SSID and passwords for your local network. And TEA, we have also a char out variable for the outs token. Once again, I'm switching back to the blink sides. Don't mix it up because here it's undefined.

Declare it a little slightly difference. But keep in mind, use this chart elements and then you're in a safe site. Then in the setup, just we making a book Blink begin with the author variable was the SSID variable and the pus. And that's all what we need after we make it run in the loop.

And then we have from proper connection to the blink website. Nevertheless, if you're using the ESP32, it's pretty straightforward. But as you can see, there are lots of other examples. When you have another microcontroller.

ESP32 FIRST CONNECTION WITH BLYNK

Let us now start with the coding part. And my approach is dead.

I'm always saving after each project my whole sketch. And I give you always the filename at the beginning of the project. And now we will start with several, one. And I also created here on file, It's called micro-credentials dot h. When you create this file and then you open your Arduino IDE, you can see yours and second top where you can omit. And in this topic, I've included my credentials in this form. Here is my SSID or my passwords and my alt key from the website, from the blink website. This is what you also can include, but you also can include it here.

In main sketch. With includes. You can add the file into the main sketch.

Don't forget to select the proper board for you. Yeah, and the board manager and the Arduino IDE to him, you can install, for example, these be 32 core. What we have to do now is we're going to the library manager and you're typing in Blink version from below the mean demand skiers the right one. When your insulin the blink. Then you also can add snow building library for the ESP 32. So let us start with domain D defines, first of all, blink several prints. Then we're defining here the template ID and the name, but I have to switch back. What's the template ID?

Afterwards, we have to include the Wi-Fi. Wi-fi clients should be included in the core. If you have not getting uncomplaining error, just go to library manager and install it. Now we've already included the blink simple USB 32 should be, I think it should be everything going doa desk setup apart. In the setup part, we now make the connection to deserve. This will be happened with the blink begin off SSID and pass isin the credentials. In the loop. We're typing in Blink run. Let's give it a try. If I've misspelled, maybe it's something I mistyped. Then compiling. Compiling. Looks good so far. Then, what do we have here now? Let's see it.

Connected, of project, the USP and toward my PC. Then we click on the indices and monitor. It's connecting. And it's connecting to my wife team. This is my temporary IP address.

```
14  BLYNK | V1.0 | 01/2022
15
16  Sources:
17  * Blynk library: https://github.com/blynkkk/blynk-library
18  */
19
20  #define BLYNK_PRINT Serial
21  #define BLYNK_TEMPLATE_ID "TMPLIXHTLyot"
22  #define BLYNK_DEVICE_NAME "ESP32LED"
23
24  #include <WiFi.h>
25  #include <WiFiClient.h>
26  #include <BlynkSimpleEsp32.h>
27  #include "my_credentials.h"
28
29
30  void setup()
31  {
32      Serial.begin(115200);
33      Blynk.begin(auth, ssid, pass);
34  }
35
```

```
Leaving...
Hard resetting via RTS pin...

---------------------------
upload complete.
```

And here we seethe blink connection is successful. You are very good. If you have some troubles, then check once again your credentials from the blinker, auth Token the template ID, and be aware of the variables for the connection. It should be in this format and then you should have and simple connection. But it's, nothing happened because we have nothing implemented, but the connection is right.

GET DATA FROM BLYNK

Now we want to make and data exchange run the web dashboard to our USP and with my new file, 0 to one, where only needs to add a few lines so that this could be happening. You can see obviously here in green dots, that means that the ESP salready connected to my dashboard. Now we're jumping above the white setup part and we typing in the blink right inside this blinker, right function. It means that the sketch will be monitored in the background if there is some changing our diet data incoming into now a weekend, simply assign a temporary variable, for example, a pinwheel you. And this will be always the same. We type in Param, this is the part of Meta which will be transferred from the dashboards to our sphere. Then we typing in as an integer because we want an integer adjust print it out. We one where you stand and print line. And then the LED is also value from 0 to one.

So we copy function here pasting in, changing to F.

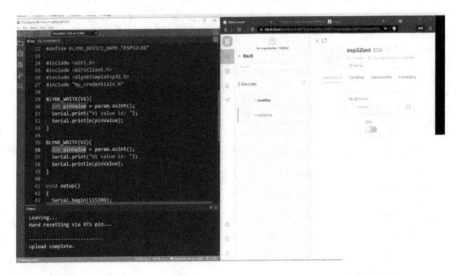

We could also leafed temporary variable PIN value because it's insights the function. And then we say ReLU is, let's give it a try. Uploads the whole sketch, and then we should make some changes. Catch his compiling and uploading. No typing errors. Uploaded completes. Then we opened a ceremony Tom, connecting to homebased. We are connected. Now. We should see when we turn on the LED, we should have an one off. Very, very good. And also here when we change the slider, we should get here some values. And as you can see it with these few lines we have here and real-time communication exchange from an Baptist sports to our ESP 72. So easy. So first, in the next project, we once now really interact with our hardware parts.

CHANGE LED STATE AND BRIGHTNESS VIA INTERNET

Now let us interact with the LED. And therefore, I would suggest if you want to follow me along, I've created a new file, three, and now we have to define at the very first beginning on Rich Pin, we have our LED and therefore integer, for example, LED pin, and it's their pinna 3232. In the setup part, we have to define pin modes.

It's called LED pin, and it's an output. Let me see if I've outputs should bean uppercases dip in O-chem. Then we could now jump into V1. And then we say, we do it because we do is to switch leaf to print earlier. For debug propose if PIN value is one, then digital rights too high. If Sarah, Digital LED pin is low, send it to the device.

It's finished, upload it. Then we're going to the serial monitor connecting the device once again, switching the camera split, we can see something. Now when I'm clicking hereon the LED, it's in front of debts. The ADD pattern. Then you can see at the serial monitor we centered one and also the LED.

Will it go on? I think the first thing works really well. Now, what do we want to do is we want to change the brightness of our LED. And therefore, I would suggest we have to add tier and other Librarian for the ESPN. When we want to make some changes to the analog rights, then we have to include here Awesome library. That means analog Write is an SP 8266 included. Here. We have to include it and it'll rights. Just download it on from the library manager. Now, first of all, we have also changed yet a digital rights.

So for example, analog Write were sent here and PGM signal, that means we can send not also, not only a digital, digital value means 0 or one, but now we can send from one to earn that 55, for example, different invidious bright LED pin. And when we want to have fits very proud to be sent to 255. Low will be here as 0. The same thing we could now apply here. For B1 means we are seeing analog Write LED pin. The pin value will be here. The value will be the variable from the pin value of sum. Now changing here.

That we also can see here the LED am a switch, but we are stuck to the brightness layer is so therefore, when our null passing the value of the pin value will be only can change values from 0 to 100, but the LED can have states from 0 to 255. And therefore, we also have here another function. And the function what we want to use is east and mapping function. So for example, we say Nu is map. This mapping function will have five integers. The first will be the variable which we put into the function that's the pinwheel here from above. And then we can see from low, from high. So our lower, the pinwheel is 0 to 100. We remember we can hear change serum to 100. This value should be changed from 0 to 255. This isn't a convenient way. Then we are writing the analog rights with the new way Lian, uploading the sketch. And then we should be able to see, hear and fading effect when we change the brightness slider upon our lab dashboard. So we have 255 different kinds of states which LED will be turned on and off. So how about my piling progress or progress? Not very far. There we go. Let's see. Uploaded. Making the hardware sets connected to homebased.

Readier refers to a website. Then LED on LDF works perfect. Led on.

If you can see here a slight change. 15%, 80 percent, Sarah will be turned off. Then I can turn it on with this slider because we 'remaking another look right? Then when I'm switching on LED switched, I need to jump to 255 and we can turn it off with the analog write brightness slider. Very nice. As you can see, simple, simple methods with brightness and switch and implemented in a real-time Internet environment.

SENDING SENSOR DATA TO BLYNK

In this project now, we want to make an exchange from their DHT 11 temperature, humidity and will be sent to our dashboard and also visualize it. Therefore, we have to add something in our templates. Templates years BY 32 LEDs.

We go to data stream and we click on Edit and we add more pins. For example, temperature. Who came is there also WAS okay, min, max, advanced sink, not daunting kids.

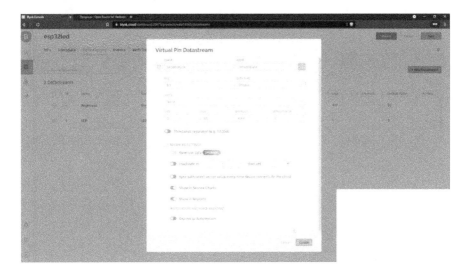

And the pin is three. Then we add a new data stream, virtual pin, which would've been for whom? 100. Some units. Let me see. Millimeter kilometer ground milligram quota seconds, Celsius. Interesting. Then. And one under default value on, looks good so far. Then we say Fitz, update the active device continuum. Switching back to our device now, before we go to dashboard, because we want to edit something, for example, drag and drop one gouge. Click on the year, some boom, we're choosing here. The temperature. Title is temperature uncongested duplicated data stream for we can choose to color, I would like a blue one.

And tier I would like to have an red one, orange safe Update device.

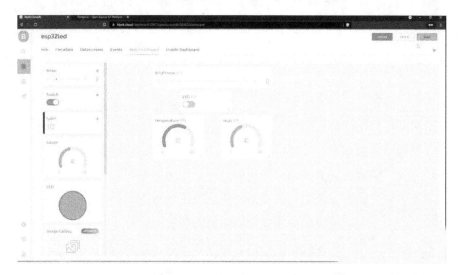

Going to my device. Espn. We have now our dashboard. But of course we haven't implemented anything in this sketch. Therefore, we are going back to false. Okay, that's better. So let us see that we get here in our sketch some data from our bed here from our sensor. We have to implement also an library, and it's called the DHT library, just downloaded through the library manager.

Then we have to define here to thinks the pin and which sensor type there is also an ADHD 22. More accuracy one. Then you have to change 20 to the pin. We have fit in the wire diagram and then we are initialize the object, the HTM with the pin and the type. And for later on, we also include here and Team in and blink time on. This is also in the core ESPN included. And now we have to jump into our setup part. We start with our VHDL and begin. And we also include in the loop that's blink timer will be run because we want to send to you on a regular basis continuously our new data to our web dashboard. And this will be assigned with our timer. So therefore, we can set in the setup timer set into volume. We can put in milliseconds defining as long and send data to blink. And this will be our own created function. Each seven seconds to timer will jump into this function and call the function. We also could do it in the loop with the Middle East, but why not using here the timeout? So going a little bit up here, I would like to use some white sand theta w. Therefore, we have to read the temperature and the humidity from our center. We're making and temporary variable. It's called Team and DHT. Temperature. If you would like to have unit Celsius, more other types, then you can type in true or for fine heights, for example. But I went to have to Celsius. Then a float atrium immunity MD BHT. That's the name of our object. Read it. Now in this temporary variable, our real-time environments sensor data will be stored. Then we're making here and logic. If it's not a number, then there is something doesn't problem. But if there is a number, if condition will be skipped. And then it's really simple to send the data to our web dashboard with say for example, V3 him, blink virtual rights, we sorry, that's the temperature. And passing the variable t, then blink. Ritter rights. V4 is too many idiom. I want for debug purpose would like to have the temperature data also in the serial monitor. And it's all we have to do here. So let's see if we got any errors in their campaigning. But I think That's all what we have to do. As you can see, it's also an simple lines of codes. Just read out the sensor data.

```
51    if(pinValue==1)analogWrite(LEDpin, 255);
52    else if(pinValue==0)analogWrite(LEDpin,0);
53
54    Serial.println(pinValue);
55  }
56
57  void sendDataToBlynk(){
58    float t = dht.readTemperature();
59    float h = dht.readHumidity();
60
61    if (isnan(h) || isnan(t)) {
62      Serial.println("Failed to read from DHT sensor!");
63      return;
64    }
65    Blynk.virtualWrite(V3, t);
66    Blynk.virtualWrite(V4, h);
67    Serial.print("tempdata: ");
68    Serial.println(t);
69  }
70
71  void setup()
72  {
73    Serial.begin(115200);
74    pinMode(LEDpin, OUTPUT);
75    dht.begin();
76    Blynk.begin(auth, ssid, pass);
77    timer.setInterval(7000L, sendDataToBlynk);
78  }
79
```

And with blink Ritter rights, we can pass values to our dashboard. Sketches uploading. We can see our setting. Turn on the 0 monotone connecting to homebased. Connected connection is there. Here we have our data tempted to 22 degrees. Perfect. As you can see, him will be updated every seven seconds. And with our temperature2200 and also your humidity and with certain date, but on the serial monitor I only printed the temperature. There we go. We have our Internet of Things device which sends data to the dashboard and we can send also data from the dashboard. To our years being ECS, it is with only around about 80 lines of code.

USE AUTOMATIZATION TO OBSERVE YOUR SENSORS

Blink offers a lot more than only sending and receiving data. There are some optimizations algorithm in the background which we can use. For example, when some values, there is a threshold from some values, then sending and they 'resending an e-mail or we get a notification on the hip. And step by the way, is also good. Downloaded it. It's the blink IoT app. And we can also create and dashboard. It's not suit with the web dashboard. All what we did so far, you can also use or make on their Android and iOS. So, but here I would like to show you what we can do with optimization. First of all, we go jump into our templates to the data streams.

For example, I would like to make your threshold from the brightness level when uncertain type of brightness level will be reached, then I wouldn't get and notification on my smartphone. So of course you can do it also with the temperature level, but it's easier with the slider to show you. Click on the first of all, we have to go to Edit, then to the brightness level.

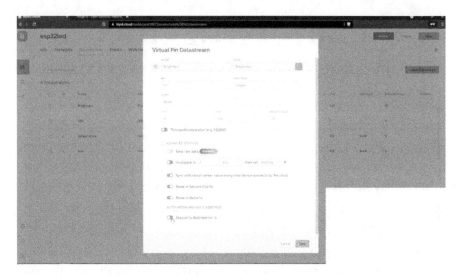

Go to Advanced scrolling down. And here we have the exposure optimization and voice assistant exposure to our optimization. Then we click available in conditions and we choosing here for example, brightness level. You see color changing range control or power switch. What available in actions? Click on Save. Click on save. Update one device continuum. Now, here, there is the optimization link missing. Just reload the page. And then we have here the optimizations. If we changed here, the data stream, then we click on optimization automations. Automations.

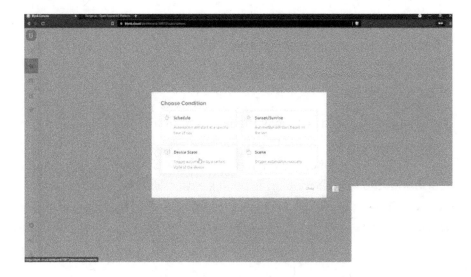

And here we have conditions, schedule on time, sunset, scene device state. And this is really handy when it comes to Internet of Things devices, for example, if you want to control some liquid levels, or you want to start some motors, some relays, etc. Really, really cool device state. For example, you canal so open windows or doors when some temperature level will be reached. But here we want to set the brightness level from our I-SPY surgeon to when. It's, let me see. Not equal, less than equal, for example, 20. Brightness control. Then send an app notification and the subject, it is too dark. Help limit, temporary, no limit. What's that? Can change those to cover. And that's it. Safe.

As you can see, we can also change here toe-mail or whatever. But I only want you to have this brightness control here. Let's jump back to our device, to our change here. Here's my device.

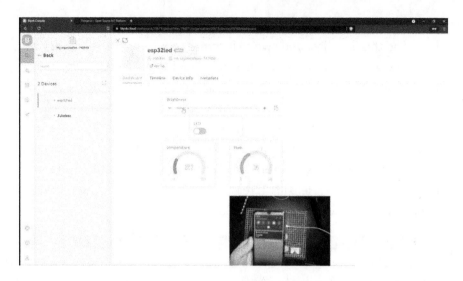

I have opened up there, blink up, but I close the app, then switching off. We are changing the brightness level. Nothing will happen. Nothing will happen. Now I go on the 20th. I got the notification from blink. It's too dark. Help. You see that instead? Instead of focus, I don't know. But here's the dark. Listen once again. Above the threshold. Going on, the knees are going below. We've got the notification. And this is also very handy when it comes to, for example, watering your plants, liquid things also with time conditions. A lot of opportunities which the blink dashboard and optimization algorithm. So far we are coming to the end of our whole project.

CONCLUSION

I would like to summarize all the learnings which we made here in this project. First of all, we created an Internet of Things device.

We are sending data from our web dashboard to our USP. For example, we can switch on the LED and also change the brightness levels. Then afterwards, we're also sending real-life sensor data toour dashboards and wish list it also in real-time on the blink website. Afterwards we edit also some optimization algorithm. For example, when the threshold is reached, then also we get notification on our smartphone. And this is really smart home oral so an Internet of devices thing was few lines of code, easy-to-use, free to use. I hope I see you in another class.

POWER SUPPLY WITH STEP-DOWN MODULE

Before we start into the voting part, I would like to discuss with you why I'm using, you know, an extra power supply.

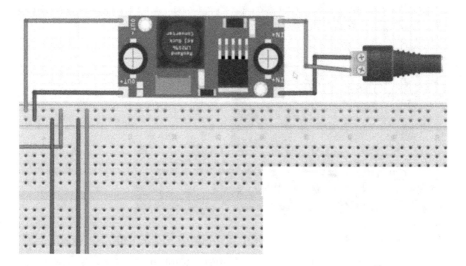

And here there is an uncoupling block where the power supply comes in to unfold. And this thing is an stepdown module from 12th World. I'm transforming into five worlds. That's, I would say, the main voltage, what I'm using for the Arduino and also for the LCD panels. So don't get confused. Here is a little error on this committee, condemned the picture. This is the plus pole, and here are the minus point and you've got two on the primary side with your12 voltage. But then with this little skill, you can adjust the whole voltage to five faults and then you can goto the breadboard and can supply the you and also the LCD matrix. Let's take a look on the other really parts here. This is the standard model, so there is an operating current from roundabout to MS. And this is a lot.

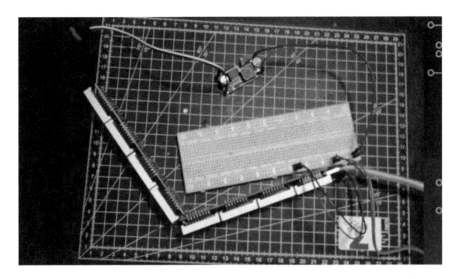

So we are really flexible in adapting our OLED modules so we can add one more panel, for example. So here I have connected two panels. Then we can add a solar panel, for example, and this gives us really a lot of flexibility in the whole developing process. So here I have the coupling plug my 12 volt power supply connecting this together. Here are the 12 volts and was this little screw. I can adjust to 12 votes to five votes, for example, to three volts. And this goes to the breadboard and I can connect the ESPN and the module, but more of the wiring part in the next project. I just want to focus why I'm using the step down model and why it's necessary or why it gives us more flexibility.

WIRING ESP32

Now we take a closer look on the whole virus. It's very easy to implement. So as we discussed before, here we have our power supply, our step Dumbledore, even on the secondary side, we are connecting it to the breadboard. Then the plus ball goes to a faithful door phone and grants to miners.

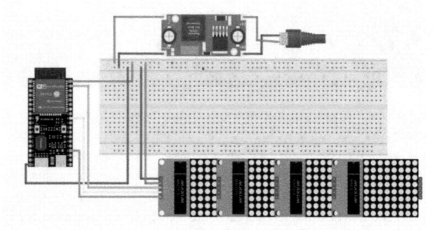

Until we have the necessity to goes to the blast pool and the ground is connected to the minus pool. Then, with three pins left, didn't clock and cease and desist, and the clock pins are already defined fixed on the pin on the USB certitude to just take a closer look on a pin out and the dimpled I connected to the pin on twenty three on the USB 32. So this could be defined later on in the original media. That's all we have to do. So switch to our tabletop. That's where you can connect the whole thing to get on. So this is the USP 82 66 comes later on my developer support for the hour doing all the USB 32. I am using an AC delivery component, so take a look.

It's a little has some little odd, a little bit different pin outs. This is necessary to know because I have you're not the grounds on the left corner as the schematic shows before. So connecting the right one, for example, to the plus and the grounds, I'm using this one. Grant Plus, and we are conducting its two parallel circuits to the breadbox, and also we are connecting your eye from the smaller Madura just for it to eight modules and the plus and minus pull of change to the top of circuits because I need another connection pin. So the first pin on the model is this year. As you can see, I think you can see it. This is see and grants. B C and then connecting to the grants, then the next pin is the green one, the green one is Dean and the import was to take a look. Twenty three so. Twenty three is on the right top. The next pin is here to see P. M.

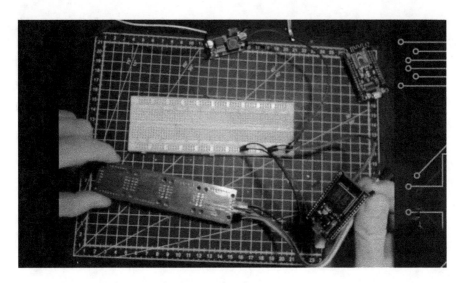

Also, take a closer look and be aware there could be little different changes in the penal odds because here in the schematics, it's different. Audits like he and my part sources suggest, goes to 15 and she says the brown one 15 to Braun. So you see, I need a little bit more space here. Fifteen girls up to. Yeah. Then the green one was twenty three, and the last one should be the clock and the clock goes to 18. It's the yellow pin. And that's all we have to do. These two cables are just two jumper cables are free because I'm used on the other one for the power supply. And that's all what we have to do to connect our whole wiring for the USP 30 to them.

WIRING ESP8266

The whole firing part for the ESPN 80 to 66 is similar to the USB 32 with your connection plug for the power supply or step down module on the secondary site. We go through the breadboard with the minus and the Plus.

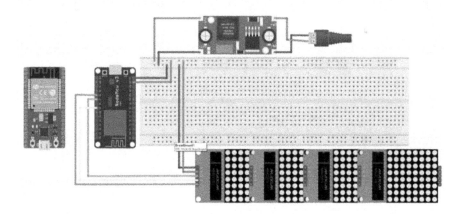

Then from the breadboard we are connecting the plus and the grounds and also C and grants to our elite emitters. Then there are three pins left in the clock. Yes, yes and clock are defined already on the note MCU. So this is connected to see as to the date and the clock, to the D5 and to the port. I've set it up to D7 and the seven port I am declaring in the original idea. These two pins is already set up on the Arduino, so there's nothing to do. Let's switch to the other camera. We have our connection black primary science with a few the secondary side. It's already set up to five worlds, and then I'm going to the perilous parallel to the breadboard then. First of all, I'm just connecting the whole thing. First of all, I have, you know, the ESPN 80 to 66, I'm going to be in and grants from the Arduino. And also I have here and similar material with four panels. So I've connected you to other jumper cables so that I can connect to the breadboard. The first pin is missing and the second is the ground layer be. Here's my bread, potassium and in the space, so it's not connected. Then the next part of the next pin is studying screen and our dean is connected to the seven on our Arduino on D7. Next thing is the see, and it's brown.

So take a look here on my actual device. It's a little bit different than on the schematic, so be aware what it's spin C-spine goes to the eight. It Estonia. And as the last pin, I have the clock pin, it's the yellow one and the clock pin goes to the five. So.

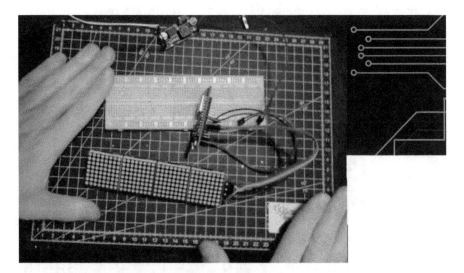

The ADHD seven and D5, OK, so there's something missing the decisive OK, so. Tick plus and finished this hour, vibrant parts with that, yes, 82, 66. That's all we have to do. And in the next part, we are focusing on the programming.

IDE SETUP

If you are new to the whole original topic, then I'm guiding you through the very first steps for setting up the whole other, you know, idea.

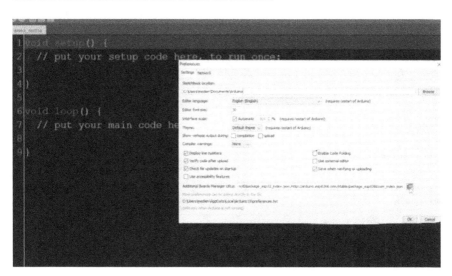

First of all, you go to file preferences because we have to set up the ESPN and we have additional board and schedules.

Just click on this small icon and therefore you have to put in to use one for the USB 3. 2 when you'reusing the to use P32 or USB 82. 66.

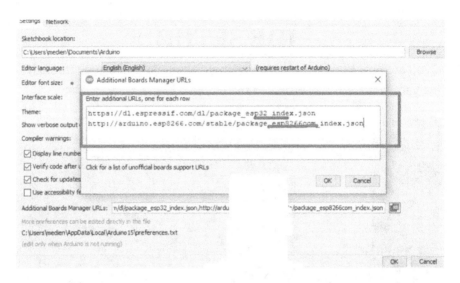

So with this declaration after us, the Arduino Eddie knows, OK, you're using this specific port, and then you can also attach some examples. And also the audio in you composed the code and the right way. OK. Just affirm this was OK. And so you have declared the whole that the right USP settings. The next point would be to go to the board manager.

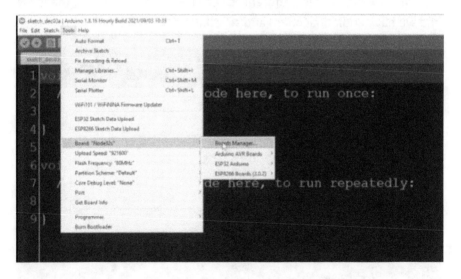

So it's under two es ports and boat manager, and then you are able to search for example, for your speed them and the four expressive systems.

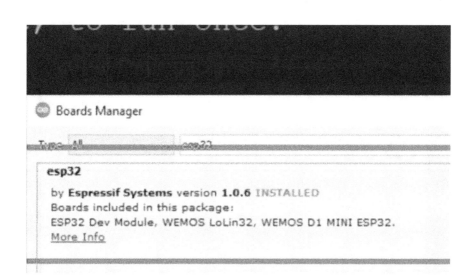

Boards Manager

Type All esp32

esp32
by **Espressif Systems** version **1.0.6** INSTALLED
Boards included in this package:
ESP32 Dev Module, WEMOS LoLin32, WEMOS D1 MINI ESP32.
More Info

You can install this version. And then you should have here and new points from boards. Yes. So two arenas and you're a different kind of use piece, and I'm using the other, you know, 32 developer port and I'm using this point. So select this one. And now I'm connecting the original wish to use sports the tongue. And when you're on the Windows machine, you can type in device manager and this dialog should open it. And then two, maybe two things can happen. First of all, here should be some devices which are not installed. Then you have to search on. I'm just going to try to add your components and install the driver. Plug in the Arduino once again and then in the order in should be somewhere here on the connection points.

And I've connected it already until you see the you know why it is necessary to know because we should know the proper ports. And I'm using the ports here. It's already defined for me for windows. Then you go to tools selecting the port ports. And now you have finished setting up the original idea for it. Use P32 and for a USP 82 66, you can go make the similar steps. So then we are ready to develop the whole programming code.

LIBRARIES AND FIRST TEXT OUTPUT

So in his first project, we are gonna setting up a whole libraries and also make the first takes the outputs therefrom. I'm creating all in each project and new folder with a new number so that you can download after each chapter, after each project, my whole quotes so that you can write Trump into the whole development process. Here I have an completely new open sketch. They were just super beginning inside, and so what I've done already is opening the folder. Once again, I have implemented or created a new file.

It's called my Ildy Matrix, and the necessary ending is the Dot H should just create a dot h with, for example, this name and reopen the Arduino idiom once again. And then you see here the idea has I'm the second cup and you we have also and you top this up. This gives us more space to structure our code. That means we have an audio file where we can put the code inside, and this will be referenced here inside the main code.

And so because we have a lot of different projects in this whole project, and therefore it's a little bit more structured and how we could how could we implement this H5? So we just go here like includes my deleted

Matrix H and now everything which is written inside this file will be all accessible in the main file. So then how could we start? First of all, setting up the ESPN 32m and I'm using, yeah, the watch dog to watch dog is an helper program, I would say, which continuously monitors the background. So if a process is or lasts longer than two or three seconds, the Arduino watchdog will opened and says, I use something not right and rebooting the system or stop the system. Therefore, I'm including the ESRB task community that should be installed already, but you have to declare it, and we are jumping into the loop and the loop. I'm resetting the wheel, for example. USP, a task we need to, and it's called reset. So that means the timer for the watchdog will be reset that each loop. So there shouldn't be any cases that watchdog will be up here, OK? This was the first step. And now jumping into the LED matrix.

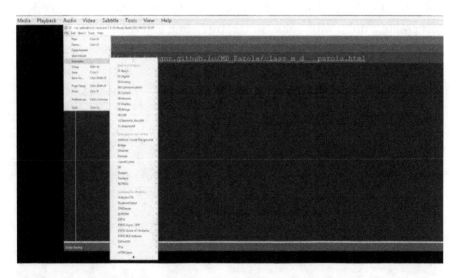

So let us focus on what we are need to set up demotic so that we can display some text on it. So it's very, very simple because we have there are some examples, libraries and examples. Coaches for is a leading matrix. And also, I give you here the proper GitHub link so that you can see how you can access all the necessary classes. First of all, we have to implement or include the proper library, and therefore we are using this M. D. Paula.

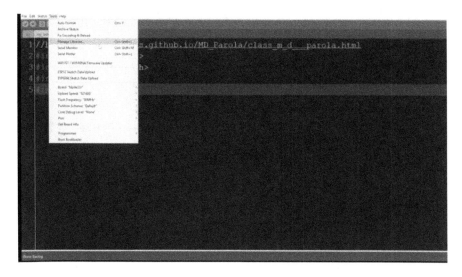

You can go to tools to manage libraries, and this dialogue needs a little time to open and after it's finished. Loading, We are typing here in empty underline, Paula.

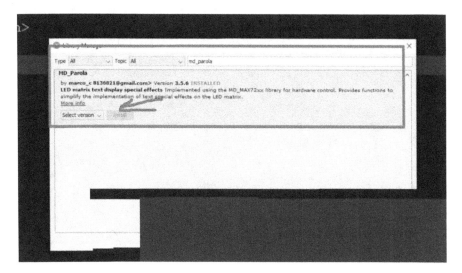

So as you can see, I've already installed it and then you can click on install and when you click on install and the second dialog will be opened and you should be asked, should I also install the MD mark 72? Of course you should. And then which is to include statements, we have set up a you idea for the LCD matrix. And as it explains, we are using the hardware type that's just defining it. And the next step will be defining the LCD module. So first of all, I'm using here four eight two eight modules, and that's why I'm declaring here for later on. We are using, for example, eight of this modules. Then you are typing, you're in it as a next step. But we. Declaring the pins, which we are connected from the original to the matrix, as we did in the 60s before, and then we are I'm calling the constructor with the barrier ruining my display. We are passing the very areas which we are declared here on, and that's all what we have to do. Then I may make here on a new function, for example, start displaying and now I'm typing in here some basic, um, some basic things to writing, some text on the display. First of all, we initializing the object. Therefore, we say my display don't begin the next one. For example, you could set the intensity of the display that will be it was my display dot set intensity and then you can see some misspelling such intensity, for example it. And each time I'm making a change of the display, I'm using my display clear. And afterwards, I can change the text on it. So, for example, display text.

```
#define HARDWARE_TYPE MD_MAX72XX::FC16_HW
#define MAX_DEVICES 4
#define CS_PIN 15
#define DIN 23
#define CLK 18

MD_Parola myDisplay = MD_Parola(HARDWARE_TYPE, CS_PIN, MAX_DEVICES);

void startDisplay(){
    // Intialize the object:
    myDisplay.begin();
        // Set the intensity (brightness) of the display (0-15):
        myDisplay.setIntensity(8);
            // Clear the display:
    myDisplay.displayClear();
}
```

But before we have to say my display points, display text and now we have you a few things, but we can. And first of all, we can say, for example, my text, then we can adjust the alignment, then to speed with when the text will be entered, for example, 80 milliseconds. There should be any pause and then we can see a scroll from the left. So that means the effect comes in from the left and also go out on the left side. Because here we could, for example, say it will be entered the text from the left side and also go outside from the to the right side or it comes from the left and goes out to the left side. So I'm using left to left, so it should be sliding through the whole display. This is my start. Up to four months, a little bit more suitable. So this is the first thing which we are using to toto display some text, but we are not finished jumping right back to our main program. It's calling a little bit down because now in the setup, we have to call it and the function starts displaying and also for debug reasons, I say, finished loading. So it's one thing is missing that we can make some changes. We have to call in the loop. If my display is animated, reset it.

```
Serial.begin(115200);

startDisplay();
Serial.println("finished loading");

}

void loop() {

  //woof woof
  esp_task_wdt_reset();

  if (myDisplay.               ()) {
    myDisplay.displayReset();
  }
```

And so the display will be also affected and also will be changed out of format. Then I'm checking the compiler if I've misspelled or mis typed anything. So it looks good. Everything is set up. It was successfully uploaded. Now we are changing the camera open to super monitor re boots. The whole thing, as we can see, finished loading And there we go. We have our sliding text from left coming in, going out to the left and it's called my text. And this was our first example to setting up the LCD matrix. Just very simple with a static text with the USPS. 32.

ADJUST THE SLIDING TEXT

In this project, we are focusing a little bit more on the details on this whole sliding aspect. I've created a new file, it's called too. So when you're developing with me and then you can use my files from the platform, just download it and you are on the right step. So switching back to my matrix, scrolling a little bit down.

So what we can do is, of course, we can change our text and just to get an overview, I'm changing the cameras so you know we can position the text. That means some should to text to somewhere stand still or should it go left to the right. Here we can change the speed, for example. I think this would be 150. Then I let the text stand at the pass, for example, to seconds. It goes in on the right and goes out to the left, then uploading the whole sketch. Sketches uploading now you see, the text comes in from the right stands still for two seconds.

This is this one and goes back to the left. So on the link on the first line, when you open this home, this website, you can see here a classist what you can do with this whole object. And you also can, for example, set it to invert the text intensifier.

```
#define HARDWARE_TYPE MD_MAX72XX::FC16_HW
#define MAX_DEVICES 4
#define CS_PIN 15
#define DIN 23
#define CLK 18

MD_Parola myDisplay = MD_Parola(HARDWARE_TYPE, CS_PIN, MAX_DEVICES);

void startDisplay() {
  // Initialize the object:
  myDisplay.begin();
  // Set the intensity (brightness) of the display (0-15):
  myDisplay.setIntensity(8);
  myDisplay.setInvert(true);
  // Clear the display:
  myDisplay.displayClear();
  //displayText(pText, align, speed, pause, effectIn, effectOut (150 langsam 100 s
  myDisplay.displayText("-EDI-", PA_CENTER, 150, 2000, PA_SCROLL_RIGHT, PA_SCROLL_LEFT);
}

Leaving...
Hard resetting via RTS pin...
```

For example, my display sits. Let's take a closer look. What was it set in that? For example, a true. Beam it up, and here you can go through this whole adjustments and to see what you can do with the Matrix and take a closer look. As you can see with inverted the whole energy matrix. So this chip should give you just a quick overview on what you can do, what

75

LCD Matrix is capable. I think there are a lot of opportunities in the next few years. We're focusing on a little bit more to interconnect more energy models and inserting graphics.

INTERCONNECT LED MODULE

In this project, we are interconnecting to LCD panels so that we have eight to eight pennies, a lot of eight. So let's check the overview. I found two panels connecting soldering together on the edges. And what I've done so far is connected load the schematic we did before, she said. The key task? Nothing special. And when I'm connecting all of the power supply, you can see.

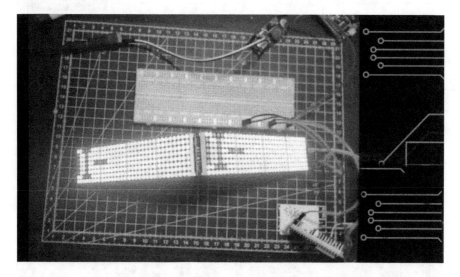

That's the last sketch will be displayed but displayed on each panel by its own. And that's not what we want. So we are focusing back onto our sketch. I've renamed and created a new one point or three, and now all what we have to do now is going to myLCD matrix changing here.

```
//https://majicdesigns.github.io/MD_Parola/class_m_d__parola.html
#include <MD_Parola.h>
#include <MD_MAX72xx.h>
#include <SPI.h>
#include <String>

#define HARDWARE_TYPE MD_MAX72XX::FC16_HW
#define MAX_DEVICES 8
#define CS_PIN 15
#define DIN 23
#define CLK 18

MD_Parola myDisplay = MD_Parola(HARDWARE_TYPE, CS_PIN, MAX_DEVICES);


void startDisplay() {
  // Initialize the object;
```

The next device to eight, then connecting the Arduino is to use sports. Uploading the sketch. Then turn on the other camera, and now it's faded in our sliding in from the left waits in the middle. Of course, here it's a little bit thick and goes out to the right. So now, as you can see, we with interconnected two panels. You can add much more panels on each side. There are some, some fields where you can connect or soldiering the things together, and then you can have the matrix and you can slide texts from each side to the other side.

PACMAN AND TEXT

Next, project file is number four, and now we want to add some graphic to the LCD matrix. Therefore, I'm going to warn the matrix file and scrolling a little bit down. And I have already converted a graphic into a hex. What is this and how you can do it, we see in later project.

I just paste in the text. So here is the whole content from, for example, in Pacman. And this indicates the frames so we can animate also our graphics. That means this graphic has six animations. You can see one picture each line. One, two, three, four, five and six. And this gives indicates how big or how large the image is. And here we have declared eight and it's an eight to eight matrix. So that means one two three four five six seven eight rows are used with this Beckman. So far so good. Now we are scrolling a little bit down and now what we want to do is we want to edit the Pac-Man. The Pacman should come inside from the left, and when it's gone, the text should be appear. And on the other side, when it's slide it through, it should come back and should eat the text and should go on the other side out. So therefore, we living in the text, but we are changing here not to scroll. We say here we are using a sprite. So that means that the effect in and effect out will be used from the Sprite. So from our new declared picture and this will be done with and second line of codes set sprite data. And now we are including the name of the the graphic. It's Pac-Man one. We are declaring the with its. It's declared three p. m. . And the third one is if payment one, I think, is this right? Yes. And then we could also make changes from the beginning and ending, but we are using the same pictureand the same adjustments.

```
0x00, 0x42, 0xe7, 0xe7, 0xff, 0xff, 0x7e, 0x3c,
};


void startDisplay() {

  // Intialize the object:
  myDisplay.begin();
  // Set the intensity (brightness) of the display (0-15):
  myDisplay.setIntensity(5);
  myDisplay.setInvert(false);
  // Clear the display:
  myDisplay.displayClear();
  //displayText(pText, align, speed, pause, effectIn, effectOut (150 langsam 100 schneller)
  myDisplay.setSpriteData(                    );
  myDisplay.displayText("-EDI-", PA_CENTER, 150, 2000, PA_SPRITE, PA_SPRITE);
  //myDisplay.write("text");
}
```

So we have to set the Sprite data and we can use also here and text, for example, we can type in. Do we know or care? So far, so good. We have here normal despite the display text and here and this line is just a static text when you would like to make a boring Alethea matrix than just type in my display. That's right. And the text. Then you have an static text to the left. OK. So let's check the compiler if something is missing in our codes. That's comma is too much. So it's uploading and we're changing the camera. Here we go. We have our Pac-Man pick. Him comes from the left.

Goes to the right. We have our text, our Lenovo displayed in the center of the Matrix. It comes in from the right and eating up our text. And this will be done with the Sprite effect out, for example. And then we see that he comes from the right side. OK. So we have now implemented and graphic with this lines of code. We set up the frame rate, also the width, and we are declared this was one statement in the stars display function.

ROCKET, BUNNY, HEART AND OTHER CONTENT

In this project, now we are implementing a few more graphics and also implement the logic that the graphics will change on a specific time in Dubai. But first of all, let's jump into a new file. It's called number five and I'm going to the LCD demographics. And now let me see. I've prepared here a lot of graphics. That's from the example from me. What I'm just pasting it to the file and we're scrolling through it so that you can see what I've done here. First of all, I set on global variable post time. This means when the text should be standstill in the middle of the center. So Pacman, we have already known this one with a second. Pacman goes purse. It's by a Pacman.

```
11 #define CLK 18
12
13 MD_Parola myDisplay = MD_Parola(HARDWARE_TYPE, CS_PIN, MAX_DEVICES);
14
15 // Pause time
16 const uint16_t PAUSE_TIME = 1000; // in milliseconds
17
18 // Sprite Definitions
19 const uint8_t F_PMAN1 = 6;
20 const uint8_t W_PMAN1 = 8;
21 const uint8_t PROGMEM pacman1[F_PMAN1 * W_PMAN1] = // gobbling pacman animation
22 {
23    0x00, 0x81, 0xc3, 0xe7, 0xff, 0x7e, 0x7e, 0x3c,
24    0x00, 0x42, 0xe7, 0xe7, 0xff, 0xff, 0x7e,
25    0x24, 0x66, 0xe7, 0xff, 0xff, 0xff, 0x7e,
26    0x3c, 0x7e, 0xff, 0xff, 0xff, 0xff, 0x7e,
27    0x24, 0x66, 0xe7, 0xff, 0xff, 0xff, 0x7e,
28    0x00, 0x42, 0xe7, 0xe7, 0xff, 0xff, 0x7e,
```

Then we have an rockets Anthony and come and hard and go away. And that's it. This is just that you see what is possible with this kind of ultimate. So now we want to handle and the change of the display a little bit more flexible. And therefore I would suggest we make a new function and it's called change display. So we are pausing here on a string. Which spreads and spreads is nothing to drink here. It's the text, and first of all, we say display my display. Yeah. And for different reasons. Print line which sprites? So then, for example, the first graphic? What is the first graphic and Pac-Man becoming one? I would suggest if we sit, which Sprite is, for example, rockets, this will be in a condition if Klaus.

```
106 };
107
108 void changeDisplay(String whichsprite) {
109    myDisplay.displayClear();
110    Serial.println(whichsprite);
111
112    if (whichsprite == "rocket") {
113       myDisplay.setSpriteData(rocket, W_ROCKET, F_ROCKET, rocket, W_ROCKET, F_ROCKET);
114       myDisplay.displayText("-EDI-", PA_CENTER, 150, 2000, PA_SPRITE, PA_SPRITE);
115    }
116 }
117
118 void startDisplay() {
119
120    // Intialize the object:
121    myDisplay.begin();
122    // Set the intensity (brightness) of the display (0-15):
123    myDisplay.setIntensity(5);
```

And if this is true, then as we did before, I can copy it and this one we say to our diplomats, I say my display, said Sprite Rockets. Dan, it's we rockets. If the rockets and the steam can cook and based on the seconds arguments, then for example, we could put a year or two, you know, research center and we have the global variable past time and we say a sprite and a Sprite, and that's all what we have to do in this function. So if which Sprite, which is passed in dysfunction and then can you handle us through all as ifs and so on and so on? I've already prepared the statements for you, so it could be all the things here and pasted in. That means we have here. The rich Sprite is Rocket Bunny, Ghost, Pac-Man, Walker Wave and Hearts IV insincerity and static text. But I'm you flexible with their hearts. Why I'm doing this This is also preparation for later on when we are passing the value of the variables from the website to the original. And we want to display different kind of things and will control this from the website. Therefore, with year on proper function, which controls us the whole graphics. OK, so far so good for the LCD matrix. Now switching back to our main file, let's have a look. So when we are, for example, going to the void setup, then we can change display rockets. Let's give it a try. What will happens? Sketches uploading since the camera. So.

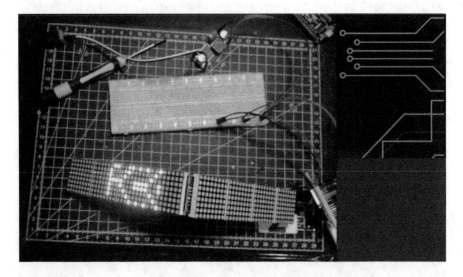

This wasn't too fast approach, we have to change something here because let's go back. We have to make a change to start this place should call it because we have here the mighty split begin. This is necessary that we can change here something. So for example, start this plan, then we may can delay this just for deeper purpose. And then we can say, for example, change disparate rockets, switching to camera. And now, as you can see, that we can change the text on the Olympics. But no, it's not very flexible. We want now create a logic and function which iterate through all the different kind of graphics. Therefore, we need to start display. Switching back to the early matrix and the start display, I changed the text of loading, then I'm saying not that here is coming in Beckman. I see. What was it? It was left, right. Scroll left. Yes, page scroll left. And it goes out also on the left side. So we're free and proper starting display, which indicates, OK, everything is loading and this will be happened here now in the loop.

We want the logic that iterates us through the hole through all the graphics. Therefore, we are using the blink without delay concept. If you're not familiar with it. Go to file examples. Digital blink without delay, you see on proper explanation. In a short summary, What is it? We are using the runtime of the script and asking in each loop is the runtime bigger than an interval, which we set up? If it's true, then do something. It's not true. Just loop through it into the main concept is in and delayed. The whole original sketch will be on hold until the delay will be finished. And that's not good because if we are setting a delay, for example, for 10 seconds, nothing else could happened on the original sketch. And that's not what we want. We want that sketch, which looping through all the time and the condition would be checked. And if the runtime is greater than an interval, then of course we should call the function so. How could we do that? First of all, we have to define two new variables global variables we thought, namely two previous models and also an interval, and this will indicate five seconds. And we are also declaring an integer and it's called count. OK, keep scrolling to the loop. No certs variable is coming and it's called current models. Now to the blink without delay logic, we see if current models minus previous models greater than the interval, then something should be happen. But before I forget this, often previous models is current bills. Now we can define our change display, for example, dark. So let us go through the logic of this concept. Current models are indicated in the loop once the previous models is in the global approach, and it's defined at zero and the interval is set at five seconds. So assume we are looping through it. We are now and two seconds. The current models has two seconds in it minus zero is not greater than the five seconds, four, five,etc. On the 60-second. For example, current Millis has six seconds. Previous models zero six minus zero is six. Six is greater than five. It's true. So the previous models is set to six seconds. Then the change display will be executed and the loop starts all over again. But now we are in the seven seconds. Current Millis now holds the value for seven seconds. Seven minus the six seconds from before it's one is not greater than the five of the interval, looping through through or through until the current model is minus the previous Millis is greater than five seconds. And as you can see, it's an really nice concept of looping through and logic and also that we can execute or something. So the next thing is we have declared on count variable. So for example, we could say if count is zero, then change display money. Afterwards, I say declare count plus incremented by one. And then we are also making his claim for parking totals.

```
//woof woof
esp_task_wdt_reset();
if (myDisplay.displayAnimate()) {
  myDisplay.displayReset();
}

unsigned long currentMillis = millis();
if(currentMillis - previousMillis >= interval){
  previousMillis=currentMillis;

  if(cnt--0) changeDisplay("bunny");

  cnt++;
  Serial.println(cnt);

}
)
```

And afterwards it's finished. But what will happened? OK, I'll see if I count one, for example, then we have to draw Rocketed to the bunny. But what happens when we are created then, for example, and posting in here do other things. Tours out of format. So now what will happened after the sixth loop through this logic? Then we have seven, what will happen with the number seven? Nothing. And therefore we have to reset the calendar every year and we say this count greater than seven. Not count is zero. So because on the sixth loop, we incremented by one. Then it's seven. And if it's seven, reset to zero and it starts all over again. So I'm going onto the top. Let's see. How is the interval? I set it to seven seconds. Maybe it's last three one slight going to the compiler. See if we misspelled something or missed something that looks good. Then we're uploading the code, switching to the camera. The rocket is sliding from the left to the right from our previous sketch. Now it's uploading and I'm excited if we have successfully implemented our logic. So first of all, we have the loading dialog. It waits five seconds. Ceremony to the rocket is the first, and this is the first one. Then the bunny is the second one. Then after the next 10 seconds, the ghosts will come, the Pacman should be the next one. There we go. The workers should follow this, you can see a lot of funny, funny elements included. Also, the wife is very nice. As the last part, we have the hearts. And then we should all over again to the Rockets. Nice one. Rocket rockets zero and one because we incremented and then we are making the silver bullet. But you get the clue what I want to show you, and therefore we have. It's now implemented on simple logic where we can iterate through our terrific.

CREATE AND DISPLAY YOUR OWN GRAPHIC LET'S GO ONLINE

The next program number is number six, and now we are focusing on how to create our own graphic for the LG matrix. Therefore, we are opening websites by the end of the 20 21 the dot matrix to come this accessible and good to use for us. So we have here on March six, we're changing the width to its Insta heights to it, and now our full potential of the creativity will be will be asked for and we are now making here and Moji, for example. It's too much. So this is my emotion. Then I can click on Generate and we get the information, what we need, but before we implement this one. This line of code, we are switching a little bit smaller the window.

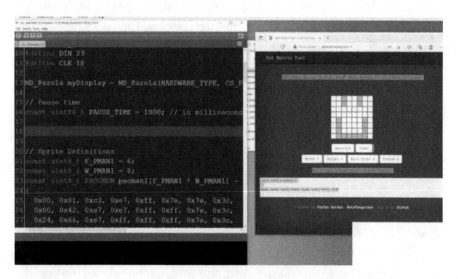

So going to my Aliadiere matrix and scrolling a little bit down, and here I will define my new constant to eight. What's it called and cooked in pasting it from the command, for example? To suck, and I'm call it more,

Jim, a emotion. And also here I'm using lower case emotion. So passing through the frames and with no first line of code, we're going to read it here and emotion posting and deleting the other half lines. But we are not finished yet. Come the end. Now we are making here some baby and tongue, so that should indicated that he shows us the tongue. Click on Generate. And with the second image, and therefore we could now create an little animation. As you can see it, you now can also edit unserved frame if you like to do that. I have enough with two friends. Some frames I change to two frames and the width is eight pixels to see there is nothing in it, but we declare it did so one two three four, five, six, seven, eight and two frames. Now I want to display and wants to take a closer look on what we are created here. Therefore, I would suggest we going through the Let's. Let's think we're going through two starts, for example, squirming a little bit down there at the start is the stance we're using. Yeah, the start function, like just full screen screaming back. I'm using here this text just for training purposes.

```
    myDisplay.begin();
    // Set the intensity (brightness) of the display (0-15):
    myDisplay.setIntensity(5);
    myDisplay.setInvert(false);
    // Clear the display:
    myDisplay.displayClear();
    //displayText(pText, align, speed, pause, effectIn, effectOut (150 langsam 100 schneller)
    //myDisplay.displayText("Loading...", PA_CENTER, 150, 2000, PA_SCROLL_LEFT, PA_SCROLL_RIGHT);

    myDisplay.setSpriteData(rocket, W_ROCKET, F_ROCKET, rocket, W_ROCKET, F_ROCKET);
    myDisplay.displayText("ARDUINO", PA_CENTER, 100, PAUSE_TIME, PA_SPRITE, PA_SPRITE);
}

void changeDisplay(String whichsprite) {
    myDisplay.displayClear();
    Serial.println(whichsprite);

    if (whichsprite == "rocket") {
```

We are editing them to the start display function. Now we have to imagine we in. Oh, gee, if energy. Copy pasted. Groaning, it's. Since the center is bright, it looks perfect to me going to the main file to start display will call it in the set up and the whole logic from iterating through the loop.

```
41  unsigned long currentMillis = millis();
42  if (currentMillis - previousMillis >= interval) {
43      previousMillis = currentMillis;
44
45      if(cnt==0) changeDisplay("rocket");
46      else if(cnt==1) changeDisplay("bunny");
47      else if(cnt==2) changeDisplay("ghost");
48      else if(cnt==3) changeDisplay("pacman");
49      else if(cnt==4) changeDisplay("walker");
50      else if(cnt==5) changeDisplay("wave");
51      else if(cnt==6) changeDisplay("heart");
52
53      Serial.println(cnt);
54      cnt++;
55
56      if(cnt>=7)cnt=0;
57  }
58  */
59
```

I am commenting on it because this is no longer needed, but the logic itself is needed a little bit later on. But now we are just want to check if our fancy emotion will be in appear on our idiomatic step from the original. It takes always a lot, a long time. So. Something is missing too many initialize for one, then take a closer look. This should be W- once again. Check if there's an error. I'll bring it back, but now I want to see it on full screen. So and now you can see it. Here is our emoji. Blinking with two frames per second shows us the tongue and goes right out of the idiomatic, as you can see. It's a funny way to implement your own graphics to the idiomatic.

ESTABLISH WIFI CONNECTION

We are starting now into a new chapter. Therefore, I've created a new file. Oh, seven.

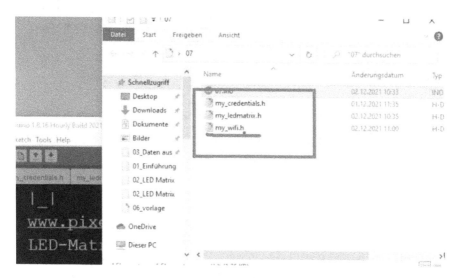

And as you can see, I've also created two new files. My wife vetoed age and those are my credentials today, as the name says, You comes in your wife, editors and you were making the logic from the connection. So let's start by opening the original idea. And now, first of all, we are including here a new library and it's called Include Wife. If you haven't already downloaded, downloaded and manage libraries, that so far all what we need. But before we have to include the older files, my credentials and also her state includes my wife itch.

```
File Edit Sketch Tools Help

10    |_|
11    www.pixeledi.eu
12    LED-Matrix Anzeige via WEB-Server | V1.0 | 12 2021
13
14 */
15
16 #include <WiFi.h>
17 #include <esp_task_wdt.h>
18 #include "my_ledmatrix.h"
19 #include "my_credentials.h"
20 #include "my_wifi.h"
21
22 unsigned long previousMillis = 0;
23 const long interval = 5 * 1000;
24 int cnt = 0;
25
26 void setup() {
27    // Serial port for debugging purposes
28    Serial.begin(115200);
```

So switching to my wife team? Let's take a look. What is your insight? Nothing. Very good. We are creating here a new function. It's called example two access points and stand the connection. We are seeing why few dots begin. And we include in the wife between function and passwords. So this is referenced as and very rude and the variables are in the credentials. And has this kind of structure that means my I. D. , for example. And you define your password, but you define this two lines, of project, into my credentials, my fancy passwords. This is the structure from these two very areas. And so we can use here the global very rules to connect to the wiki. Yeah. And then we're making on while their status is not connected. So it's the process of the connection we are seeing here for the purpose server and connecting to I feel and I'm hearing today from June 2nd, for example, then after a few seconds, the connection should be established.

```
void connectToAP() {
  //connection
  WiFi.begin(ssid, password);
  while (WiFi.status() != WL_CONNECTED) {
    delay(1000);
    Serial.println("Connecting to WiFi..");
  }
  Serial.println("WiFi connected");
}
```

And then we let us print out the local IP, which Spear will get from the from your router or your access point. Later on, we are setting up a static IP, but now we just want to check if everything works well. So let me think if we something missed, just check the compiler. I think notes, but we have to make the connection after the server begin, for example. Now we can connect to access points and we can say delay the 100 and then the connections would be established. The IP address should be written on the server monitor and then the display can start. So let's uploads the codes so that a code is uploaded open.

```
31  delay(100);
32
33  server.begin();
34  Serial.println(
35  }
36
37  void loop() {
38
39    //woof woof
40    esp_task_wdt_re:
41    if (myDisplay.
42      myDisplay.dis
43    }
44
45  /*
46    unsigned long c
47    if (currentMill
48      previousMillis = currentMillis;
```

```
Connecting to WiFi..
Connecting to WiFi..
192.168.178.61
finished loading
```

The ceremony don't always see connecting to WiFi. Now we are seeing the IP address and finished loading and the ability matrix is also showing this the start up from the from. How is it called to start this function? OK, so far so good. We now established a Wi-Fi connection, and in the next projects, we will go further on to set up bits of.

SPIFFS

Let's talk about this in this project now. We have a new project fi. No, no, it's. And also I'm included a new age by my text dot h. Opened the original idea, and now in the main file we have to add and the new library, it's called spivs. Dot H.

```
 7    | | ) | |> < _/ |  _/ | | |
 8    | ._/|_/_/\_\__|_|\_|\_|\_,|_|
 9    | |
10    |_|
11    www.pixeledi.eu
12    LED-Matrix Anzeige via WEB-Server | V1.0 | 12 2021
13
14  */
15
16  #include <WiFi.h>
17  #include <esp_task_wdt.h>
18  #include <        .h>
19  #include "my_ledmatrix.h"
20  #include "my_credentials.h"
21  #include "my_wifi.h"
22
23  unsigned long previousMillis = 0;
24  const long interval = 5 * 1000;
25  int cnt = 0;
```

And now we are able to save content on the flash memory. Therefore, we created a new file. And I fear insert a little bit. Now let's go through the things constant trial data.

```
1  const char*  datei   = "/meintext.txt";
2  // zum Auslesen und Darstellen des textes für die LED-Matrixleiste
3  #define BUF_SIZE 75
4  char message[BUF_SIZE] = ".";
5  bool newMessageAvailable = true;
6
7  void deleteTextfile(){
8
9  }
10
11 void speichereWert(String meingrandioserText){
12
13 }
14
15 //für die Website
16 String checkTextexists(){
17
18   if (SPIFFS.exists(datei)) {
```

The data is declared with an file name. It's necessary that you ate the flesh and the flesh. And this isn't fun, so we are only adding one information to this file. That means, for example, the text what we are refereeing later on from the website to the demographics. We're sitting on the flash memory in this file. When we are overwriting the file, we are deleting before to file and creating a new one. So only one information in this text file. Then we are setting a buffer size and also an global variable message with this buffer size because this is a global very, very excess. Then later on, the saved messages don't we have and delete text file? Then we starting with deleting the files that you get an overview and how you can start with the spivs. We just type in spivs. Don't remove the data file name and then we're seeing delay, for example, 100s. But first of all, we are not ready to use this spiff because we have to initialize it in the set upfor scrolling down. And before we're connecting to the access point initialize the Smiths and this will be happened with spivs to begin and we wrap this up. And if conditions so if Smith's begin is not indicated with this one is not going very well, then we are seeing serial line.

```
File Edit Sketch Tools Help

22
23 unsigned long previousMillis = 0;
24 const long interval = 5 * 1000;
25 int cnt = 0;
26
27 void setup() {
28   // Serial port for debugging purposes
29   Serial.begin(115200);
30
31   //Initialize SPIFFS
32   if(!SPIFFS.begin()){
33     Serial.println("ERROR SPIFFS");
34     return;
35   }
36
37   connectToAP();
38   delay(100);
39
40   startDisplay();
```

And we're on this return. OK, so far, so good. Now we are able to remove and create files. Let's go through on spacing what it means, for example, safe. On safe text, for example. And also, this means that it's a peer group that came. Where we are at the time. Okay. Safe text and we are passing my fiancee texts. OK. Now what we are doing at the very first thing is we are delete, text, file and now with file, this spivs dot open the name, which is declared in the time since comma and the W we are seeing we are creating the file. If it's not existing, that's what we want now with file dot print. We are passing the string and we are closing it. And now for deeper purpose, I say data on string. There with the text. My fiance texts. It's great, it's stuck. OK, then we seen a super monitor, what is created in which file and this function I already insert is for a little purpose. It takes if the text exists, that means spoof X exists and if so, then it will be iterate through each character printed or posted through and string and then returned the string. And if nothing is saved, then it returns and falls. We are. But sticklers in string. We use this later on.

```
28    ausgabe += (char)file.read();
29    }
30    file.close();
31    return ausgabe;
32    }
33    else return "     ";
34 }
35
36
37 //für die Darstellung auf der LED-Matrix-leiste
38 void selectText(void){
39
40    File file = SPIFFS.open(datei, "r");
41
42    //zurücksetzen
43    for( int i = 0; i < sizeof(message); ++i )
44      message[i] = (char)0;
45
```

And also here we have select text. It's the same logic, but we use it in other contexts that it means every time we are calling the select text function, the global variable message will get the safety data. And so because I'm not using here some object orientated approaches, we are making us here on function when we call this void function. The message the global message for will get the text from the flash memory. You can go through the dark, the code lines. It's just opening the file iterate. First of all, reset the whole, the whole variable and then putting out the text and setting the new text to correct uncorrected file. That's all what happens here. And yes, but now we want to test our function if this works very well for us, and therefore I would suggest we go back to our main file. Go on going a little bit down to the loop. Yes, we are taking a look. And in the loop file, for example, we say save texts and we are passing a string millis. To so making a little delay, for example, one second, then afterwards, we're seeing select texts. Why are we doing that? This is our lower our function, which reference the safe text to our global of error message. And then we said zero print line message and delay one second. And now off, it shoots the ceremony to give us or save every second runtime in Millis. The next second, it should print it out to save value and next loop the next Milly's should be saved. Let's check the compiler. Aha. Next, tapping around the text file. So the third try if something is missing or misspelled, you see a lot of errors. Now I should implement an error counter here. Error count number for. Number five is also here. I so I hope you have since copied my typo errors. This yeah, so but now we are uploading the sketch. So going back to the main file so that we can see what we are doing here will bring the ceremony time connecting to the wife. Everything works well. Ah, OK, here. So let's see, then I'm passing here a little bit.

So first of all, here safe text, the Middle East Front will be saved onto my texts. Here are the Middle East value. After one seconds, the select text will be invoked and in this very own dysfunction, the spivs will be read and passed through the global very message and this will be print out and so each sitcoms and Millis will go through. Of course, each two seconds because one second will be delayed for saving text and then for the printing text. And so as you can see the saving and reading into this, this works very well.

SPIFFS DATA UPLOADER

In this project, now we are setting up an data upload after that, you spin because we are saving the index item in our website and cease-fires to The Smiths, to the flash memory and the web server, then loading the data from the spieth's and pass it to the browser.

But before we have to set up this tools, so I've already installed it, you can see this is a data uploader. It's not the same as this catch uploader.

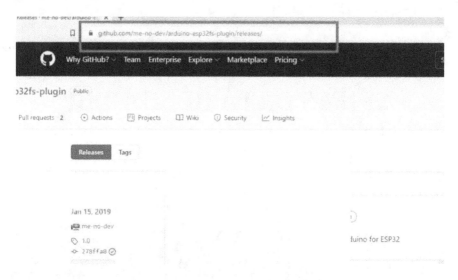

So therefore we go to the following usual GitHub site plug in release. Be aware don't load the source code. You need to be sorted to AF-S file, just download it. Then we unzip the whole thing and now you have to go to the following path. You go to, for example, and when you are on the Windows machine. Good to see your user username. Then you go to documents, go to Arduino and this is the desired path.

So once again, see if you use your username documents, Arduino, and this folder may not create a new machine. Then just create tools with an s and past passing in and copy the file, which were already downloaded and don't get mislead. You see here the whole oops, the whole the whole path.

It's called tools, ISP and once again tool without A. And there is the chop file then restarts the whole Arduino idea. And when you're restarted Rinaldi, then you should have other tools here. This data upload on this data upload unknown. So, for example, I have my folder.

This is the folder nine of this object from this project, and now I have a new folder. It's called data to have to be written. Exactly. Was this four characters? And in this folder, everything what is included in this folder will be uploaded when I click on here and say data uploader and what we have in here. We are dealing on project later on. But this should give you just an overview on how to install the bits, upload on and when you want more information, I recommend you the following URL. I can copy and paste it into this file onto the nine file sifting up the spoof because this is really necessary when we are dealing now.

This this whole up server topic and also for the SB to 66, it's just a different kind of useful just for data upload and then you find the right files, but it's the same location on your machine. And as you can see if your tools one, four, three, two and one four to eighty two sixty six. One more thing to add here is when you have opened to certain monitor, you can't upload the files. So be aware that the Arduino on the EDI hasn't opened the ceremony door. Then you can upload the spivs file.

WEB SERVER FOR THIS PROJECT

Let us set up the VIPs server on the ESP new project file number nine, and we have here a new folder data, as we discussed before, just double click on it and you can see three new files. One is an index. Hotmail is our website. We have jQuery because I like to use it when it comes to editing on the client side and also on styluses this file for formatting the website. I would suggest we start with the Index Auto ML and I am using Notepad Plus Plus to edit it, but any other editor will be good.

So simple structure, a simple HDMI structure. We have HD wirtek and had to use the headline here. I'm defining that we are also accessible with a mobile device. Here I am linking the CAC file and the J. Crew file, and here I'm also defining and Aliadiere matric shead line. That's it for the first step. Nothing more to it.

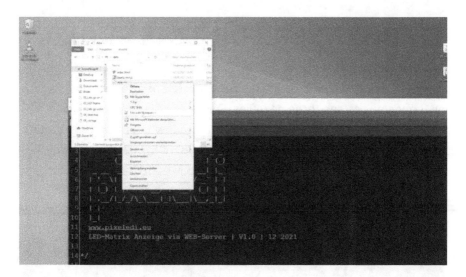

Take really just a plain cheek profile. And in the CAC file, I've added some buttons, some radial button and a little bit of blah blah.

```
17      border: none;
18      border-radius: 4px;
19      color: white;
20      padding: 10px 25px;
21      text-decoration: none;
22      font-size: 20px;
23      margin: 2px;
24      cursor: pointer;
25  }
26  .button2 {
27      background-color: #f44336;
28  }
29
30
31  .radiobuttons{
32      width:100px;
33      margin: 0 auto;
34  }
35
36  .infotext{
37      font-size:0.7em;
38      position: relative;
39      display:block;
40      color:silver;
41  }
42
43  input{
44      height:60px;
```

We are using these classes later on. So first of all, a first step connects the S Pen to the USB port and uploading the first to face. It's really necessary because I regularly forget to upload the sketch data and not the sketch to the depths of a data you see. Here are the things are uploaded now they are finished. So once again, do not forget it's not the sketch uploader, it's the data uploader. I also a mis interprets these two things on a regular basis. But no, let us focus on the setting up the web server before we jump into our main file. And we are adding here some new libraries, a lot of new libraries.

```
10    |_|
11    www.pixeledi.eu
12    LED-Matrix Anzeige via WEB-Server | V1.0 | 12 2021
13
14 */
15
16 #include <WiFi.h>
17 #include <AsyncTCP.h>
18 #include "ArduinoJson.h"
19 #include <HTTPClient.h>
20 #include <                    r.h>
21 #include <WiFiClientSecure.h>
22 #include <esp_task_wdt.h>
23 #include <SPIFFS.h>
24 #include "my_text.h"
25 #include "my_ledmatrix.h"
26 #include "my_credentials.h"
27 #include "my_wifi.h"
28
```

```
Leaving...
Hard resetting via RTS pin...
```

Then I'm pass copy paste. You need async participle. How do you, Jason HTP client is P Austin Web Server and wifely client secure just um on the library. Search for each of them. We are now need this one, but later on we also need this for libraries as well. OK, then I would suggest we jump back to my wife team and we are beginning to set up the web server and we are seeing async web server server tea with the ports. And now what I'm doing, I'm setting and static IP address. First of all, I say IP address local IP one nine two one six eight one seven eight 50 50 because on the Range 230, it's dynamically foreign from other devices in my home network and therefore I use number50 when I'm setting up the gateway. The subnet I come play down into what you can insert here and also primary DNS and secondary DNS.

```
AsyncWebServer server(80);

IPAddress local_IP(192, 168, 178, 50);
IPAddress gateway(192, 168, 178, 1);
IPAddress subnet(255, 255, 255, 0);
IPAddress primaryDNS(8, 8, 8, 8);    //optional
IPAddress secondaryDNS(8, 8, 4, 4);  //

void connectToAP() {
  // Connect to Wi-Fi
  WiFi.begin(asid, password);
  while (WiFi.status() != WL_CONNECTED) {
    delay(1000);
    Serial.println("Connecting to WiFi..");
  }
  Serial.println(WiFi.localIP());
}
```

```
Leaving...
Hard resetting via RTS pin...
```

You see, it's optional, so how you get the information for your network, for example, windows type in CMD. Yeah, then you can. I'm going through the command prompt and now you can type in IP config, for example. So a little bit in now, you can see it, here are.

```
Drahtlos-LAN-Adapter LAN-Verbindung* 10:

   Medienstatus. . . . . . . . . . . : Medium getrennt
   Verbindungsspezifisches DNS-Suffix:

Drahtlos-LAN-Adapter LAN-Verbindung* 11:

   Medienstatus. . . . . . . . . . . : Medium getrennt
   Verbindungsspezifisches DNS-Suffix:

Ethernet-Adapter Ethernet 2:

   Medienstatus. . . . . . . . . . . : Medium getrennt
   Verbindungsspezifisches DNS-Suffix:

Drahtlos-LAN-Adapter WLAN:

   Verbindungsspezifisches DNS-Suffix: fritz.box
   Verbindungslokale IPv6-Adresse . . : fe80::755d:de36:e2da:ec54%9
   IPv4-Adresse . . . . . . . . . . : 192.168.178.20
   Subnetzmaske . . . . . . . . . . : 255.255.255.0
   Standardgateway . . . . . . . . . : 192.168.178.1

Ethernet-Adapter Bluetooth-Netzwerkverbindung 8:

   Medienstatus. . . . . . . . . . . : Medium getrennt
   Verbindungsspezifisches DNS-Suffix:
```

Is my IP address, my local IP address from the computer? You also can see here the subnet and gateway and this two values you're entering into a u in to these two lines the gateway into subnet. That's all you have to do to setting up and local IP address goods. Then we need switching back to the main file. Let me see yes to the main file schooling a little bit down. And before we're connecting to the access points, we have to set up. The fixed IP address was WiFi config. We are referring the local IP, the Gateway, all these very areas, which we are defined before. So we are stick into the set up because now we are setting up the rest, the rest from the depths of debt for a few, a few lines. Seven. So what is going on here? Yeah.

```
40    return;
41  }
42
43  // Configures static IP address
44  if (!WiFi.config(local_IP, gateway, subnet, primaryDNS, secondaryDNS)) {
45    Serial.println("STA Failed to configure");
46  }
47
48  connectToAP();
49  delay(100);
50
51  server.on("/", HTTP_GET, [](AsyncWebServerRequest * request) {
52    request->send(SPIFFS, "/index.html", String(), false, processor);
53
54  });
55
56
57
58  startDisplay();
```

This can lead silver on the root level. That means when I'm entering now, the one nine two one six eight one seven eight to 50 on the browser. Then this line will, will, will, will be called. And this means OK. The request the web server sense from the index Hotmail to the browser. And that's it. That's what we are seeing here on this line. And also, we can add the ceasefire. It's necessary we have to load via the server. That means statistics until we have to declare this is this file. And don't forget if the type of term of the documents and as a last point, we also at the J. Crowley. And as the last point we see, we are sort of started on the service should begin and out of that, we are not finished yet because you can see here space is loaded. We are refereeing the index. html as a string. And we have here something else also called this this process of function, switching back to my wife team and we are declaring here there was a protest song function. What this is for, I'm dealing a little bit later on. Now we just declare it with nothing in it. We come to them. It's a little bit later back home. OK. So was this a few lines of code was declaring and fixed IP address? This is, of course, optional, but it's a more convenient

105

way if you have always the same IP address. And with setting up the IP address and with just a few lines, we have set up the web server. I hope successfully, if the compiler hasn't got any errors for me, so looks good to me. The whole sketch is uploaded or is uploading, then we are opening our browser window and typing in the IP address, which we are defines before, just with a little bit. If everything is on, yeah, then we are hitting enter. And while this is our fancy new website based on the USP Epsilon, it's working very well. Just make and short recap what we've done now. So we have here and fold our data in this folder is our index, Hotmail and status as where this websites made. Then we are uploaded the whole thing to The Smiths on the USPS.

So too, we declared and fixed static IP address. And with this few lines, we said loads from disputes, spoofed index, Hotmail and also the style and jQuery out demo.

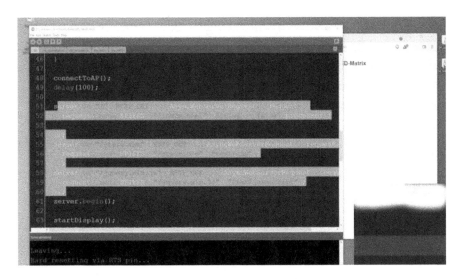

So each time I hit enter this few lines will call it and process and pass me the HD Mail file, and I can congratulate you to set it as you set it up. The first web server on an ISP and in the next projects, we are going a little bit more into detail how we can get and Rafah variables through the server and still websites.

HTML INPUT UND GET-REQUEST

In this project, now we want to focus on the websites and the website, we are creating an input field and in this input field, when we hit a button, the text should be sent via cheek area. We are getting a request to the Arduino. So how could we implement this? I've created a new project folder on the button, clicking onto the data, opening the index Hotmail with Notepad, for example. And now I want to enter some the input fields, so I am typing in here and you diff then adding here and label, for example, the label for I call it, text. Text, Ley burn and I make a line break. And here we are defining the input. No, the inputs. When you call it it, it it takes. Then we give them an idea and that we can exit it later on with Jake Crary and the type is fixed. Well, you know, it's no blank closing, it's line break, so this will make an input field. But on this input field, nothing will happen. So therefore we atheist some buttons or one button, you call it item, for example, or. Submit, however, to recall it. Text and text. Text and text from Dan Klos is putting a button send, and I think

107

I called it, and now I make on click function and Eston Name says when we click on this button that the JavaScript function, which I am now entering does something need to get, for example, will be called, then show on and the matic's and closing the button tick. OK, so let's see what we've done so far. Clicking on tools, sketch data.

Upload on. When it's not finished loaded, as you can see him, just wait a little bit. Now it's finished loading entering. No, it's not 60. It's 50. Was it 50? It was 50. Once again, I'm often too impatient. Now it's finished loading. So we can see our input field and our new created button. So and now we want to it's now the logic that we can send and pass text when we click on the button that it will be passed to the speaker. So what can we do now? First of all, let us define here the function subnets gets. Oops. No. And in this function, we say we want the text from the input fields and we say, create, this is very easy. First of all, let us define the variable and then we say the law was the hashtag and the text we are with the hashtag. It referenced to the idea and then we say thought Well, and now we have stories to text from the input field, and now we're creating a variable. I'm explaining right now what I'm doing here. So a little text. So for example, when we have this, you will then indicating with a question mark, we can define a variable, for example. Text ist, here is my new text.

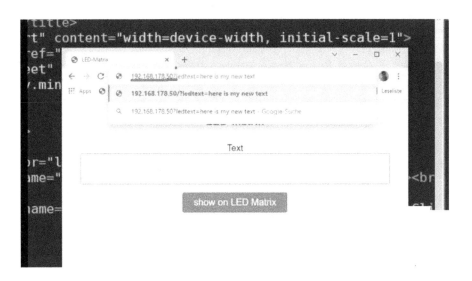

So this is the URL which is opening the whole website then was the question mark and variable is indicated. This is called text and then was the following part we can refer and passing here some text at some venues. And this is what we've done so far. That means with any text we say this is a variable and we're passing them the content from the input field. That's what we did so far. We can put this on the console, in the browser. And the next thing is we are. Making the actual get request we are seeing here the other and function data, but this is only fort's not really used here because nothing to do so we can't send and get requests to the USP that GSP does something and give suspect some information, and this data will be stored into the variable data. But we're only sending data. So there is nothing to do for us here. But you get the clue what we can do here and the other way also you can oops. You can make and get requests on a piece of this server makes the whole calculation of the really heartrate, intensity calculations, gifts, the risks of back and this this callback will be stored in the data, for example. OK. Safe uploading the news data uploads. Then here know we have our websites then waiting that the ISP started all over again. Just wait a little bit longer. OK, then right click. Then you have here and text, for example. Inspect. We have here to console you on the right side.

Then you can click on console. And now when we're typing here. My get requests, for example, and click show on Lady Matrix. We are seeing here that you usual is passed, Kosha looks good to me so far. Now we have set up the site from the website that everything is placed and coded very well, and in the next step, we are focusing on how to get the get parameter on the original site.

GET PARAMETERS ON THE ARDUINO

Now we are implementing the get request on the Arena site. I've created a new project folder number 11, so let us open this file. Don't get confused with the numbers. I always explain at the beginning of each project on which project I will work so that you can follow me along step by step. So now we want to get the request saved to the spiff, and then I'll read this piece in the loop. This will be the main task in this project. First of all, we are going into our main sites and going to the server on line. So let me see. There we go.

```
43   // Configures static IP address
44   if (!WiFi.config(local_IP, gateway, subnet, primaryDNS, secondaryDNS)) {
45       Serial.println("STA Failed to configure");
46   }
47
48   connectToAP();
49   delay(100);
50
51   server.on("/", HTTP_GET, [](AsyncWebServerRequest * request) {
52       request->send(SPIFFS, "/index.html", String(), false, processor);
53       //make a function which get the request
54       checkParams(request);
55   });
56   server.on("/style.css", HTTP_GET, [](AsyncWebServerRequest * request) {
57       request->send(SPIFFS, "/style.css", "text/css");
58   });
59   server.on("/jquery.min.js", HTTP_GET, [](AsyncWebServerRequest * request) {
60       request->send(SPIFFS, "/jquery.min.js", "text/javascript");
61   });
```

So whenever there isn't, get to it first we could to make function, which gets the request. As you can see, we get here on request with the following definition. So, for example, we could create problems and refer the requesting my wife team. For example, we created here and new function of check terms, and I'm copying this one. I think the server pasting it to the new function and then I say requests has PARAM. And now I can see any data, for example, that let me see.

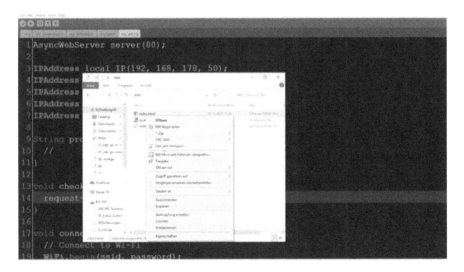

That's up 11 data indexed at the moment, and I declare it here in the usual text. If I use something else, for example, then I could get this was his parameter do, for example. So but in an if statement, so if the web server has this parameter or we get this parameter, then I have access to the venue of the get it done. And it gets put on and. With texts and to get to the value, an object, I see value, but no one does this and nothing will happen. Just gets the value. And now we say safe, safe text. Safe texts, and now it's safe.

So that means once again, if we open our website, if we hit the button we are making and get the request, which Jake really like, here we are sending the text from the input field via us and go and get requests to the other involved. The Arduino gets here. Aha. OK, he's regressed. Since then, we are calling the chicken parm function and refereeing the request object. And here we are asking and we are making an if condition is the request or has to permit texting it, when so then please save us the text. Kim, so far, so good.

```
     // Configures static IP address
43   if (!WiFi.config(local_IP, gateway, subnet, primaryDNS, secondaryDNS)) {
44     Serial.println("STA Failed to configure");
45   }
46
47
48   connectToAP();
49   delay(100);
50
51   server.on("/", HTTP_GET, [](AsyncWebServerRequest * request) {
52     request->send(SPIFFS, "/index.html", String(), false, processor);
53     //make a function which get the request
54
55   });
56   server.on("/style.css", HTTP_GET, [](AsyncWebServerRequest * request) {
57     request->send(SPIFFS, "/style.css", "text/css");
58   });
59   server.on("/jquery.min.js", HTTP_GET, [](AsyncWebServerRequest * request) {
60     request->send(SPIFFS, "/jquery.min.js", "text/javascript");
```

And now we want for mapping purpose, as I always say, wants to get the text here on the Syrian monitor, for example. So I'm a kingdom delay here. Then our global function select text. You can remember select text is therefore that's not safe. Text, select text. This function will open disputes from my the data on my text and read all the content and save it to the global variable message. And the next point we're seeing is Syria print line message. OK. I think this should work. So the scenario will be we are opening our website, typing something in hit the button. The text will be referred to our, you know, we'd be saved and will be read on the Syrian monitor. Let's see if the compiler has errors or not. OK. Song everything should be fine. Now let's upload the file. Here's two websites from now opening the ceremony to finish loading and now we are taking the browser. I am refreshing and decide. So this was the last content I saved in this piece. Here I see the Reno Spiced Toast from website. Click on show sent. You see here it will be perfectly saved. Data mining text with the text Arduino SPIVs is created and now in the loop. It's every second will be read from this piece. Now here my new text showing any demographics and the text will be deleted, created new and the new text. And so we are passing. We are get new data to the ISP and saved it to our spoofs. The main reason why we go to detour about this is that we have now and multi-user element, because now I can also open the website on my smartphone, for example. So let's see and go on.

And I can put you down just from smartphone. Send it with a spelling error, and you can see it also works from here. That means later on, when we are setting up the whole website, the text will also be shown on the website so that always the last enter text will be saved on the ISP.

PASS TEXT FROM WEBSITE

And this project now with the number 12 from the project folder, we want to change the text now to our elder matrix from the website, so we've prepared. Now a lot of things, so it should be done very easily. Let's open the new project file and now we are here, it's in the main file and with the check pass, we have successfully entered the text on safety from the website to our ISP speeds. So I'm just checking the loop in the loop. I am deleting everything out except the task from the USP. And also this two lines, three lines should be included because then the display will be changed if something is changing. OK, so we already have implemented, if you remember on the my text and function, not into my matrix and function down there where I don't change display. Here we go. Then we have the different kind of options. And here I am, creating a new one, for example.

```
150
151     else if (whichsprite == "walker") {
152         myDisplay.displayText("ARDUINO", PA_CENTER, 100, PAUSE_TIME, PA_SPRITE, PA_SPRITE);
153         myDisplay.setSpriteData(walker, W_WALKER, F_WALKER, walker, W_WALKER, F_WALKER);
154     }
155     else if (whichsprite == "wave") {
156         myDisplay.displayText("ARDUINO", PA_CENTER, 100, PAUSE_TIME, PA_SPRITE, PA_SPRITE);
157         myDisplay.setSpriteData(wave, W_WAVE, F_WAVE , wave, W_WAVE, F_WAVE );
158     }
159     else if (whichsprite == "heart") {
160         myDisplay.displayText("ARDUINO", PA_CENTER, 100, PAUSE_TIME, PA_SPRITE, PA_SPRITE);
161         myDisplay.setSpriteData(heart, W_HEART, F_HEART , heart, W_HEART, F_HEART );
162     }
163         (whichsprite == "text") {
164         myDisplay.displayText(message, PA_CENTER, 100, PAUSE_TIME, PA_SPRITE, PA_SPRITE);
165         myDisplay.setSpriteData(heart, W_HEART, F_HEART , heart, W_HEART, F_HEART );
166     }
167 }
```

Deleted text, because I just want to refer to the text, and now I'm passing the message to global variable and so that I always gets the actual value from the saved spoof, I'm calling the select texts. It's it's called select texts. Select texts, yes, select text. So with calling the select text function, I'm always getting the new and updated content from my specified. And now with existing or refereeing the message variable, we get also the actual text when we are calling and edit text. But I don't want and Smith's just only the text, and this is called P a scroll left. And also here's a scroll left. OK, so we are added to the change display now. What we are doing is we are adding our poems and we are seeing the has the function as and called backand returns a one parameter. So that means after the next projects, we can enter all our parameters, for example, rocket and if request, for example, rockets. Then we can save rockets and also we have to return the rockets. So we have a little more flexible way to check the parameters and also get yeah and string return. So remember, where do we call the chicken? At the very first beginning here and now, we are making two things with calling checkpoints. First of all, we are saving the text the parameter from the request.

```
46    }
47
48    connectToAP();
49    delay(100);
50
51    server.on("/", HTTP_GET, [](AsyncWebServerRequest * request) {
52      request->send(SPIFFS, "/index.html", String(), false, processor);
53      //make a function which get the request
54
55    });
56    server.on("/style.css", HTTP_GET, [](AsyncWebServerRequest * request) {
57      request->send(SPIFFS, "/style.css", "text/css");
58    });
59    server.on("/jquery.min.js", HTTP_GET, [](AsyncWebServerRequest * request) {
60      request->send(SPIFFS, "/jquery.min.js", "text/javascript");
61    });
62    server.begin();
63
64    startDisplay();
```

And also we are getting big and strong so we can use now the code pick from the Czech poems to change the display. Because Change Display will get also on string. And when we have passing the text, it's calling this line, so it shows us the message which is globally saved and to the abyss. And the scrolling left to right with one second pause. Once again, with this line, we're making two things we are saving the text to dismiss getting callback and changing the display. So much to theory. Let's check the compiler if everything is right and send it to our other, you know, no errors occur. But before we go further on, let us check the start up to start display. Here we have the emoji inside. We delete this one. I want your Justin loading and texts, and this will be from left to left a scroll left. So then where if you scroll left to left safe uploads, we don't need to update our sketched as data uploads because we have nothing changed on the website. We just changed the code from this catch. So let us change the camera then. Text is uploading.

116

```
     0x04, 0x02, 0x01, 0x02, 0x04, 0x08, 0x10, 0x20, 0x40, 0x80, 0x40, 0x20, 0x10, 0x08,
};

void startDisplay() {
  // Intialize the object:
  myDisplay.begin();
  // Set the intensity (brightness) of the display (0-15):
  myDisplay.setIntensity(5);
  myDisplay.setInvert(false);
  // Clear the display:
  myDisplay.displayClear();
  //displayText(pText, align, speed, pause, effectIn, effectOut (150 langsam 100
  myDisplay.displayText("loading...", PA_CENTER, 150, 2000, PA_SCROLL_LEFT, PA_S
}

void changeDisplay(String whichsprite) {
  selectText();
```

Looks good. Let's see now we have already passed to start display phase now the loading text is so long on the sliding through the LCD matrix until we change the text on the website. Let's open the website. So now I'm typing in, for example, a text from website clicking and here we have our text from the website. Perfect, perfect. And this is all what we want to do in this example. In the next example is when we are refreshing the website that this last safe text will also be shown on the website.

117

SHOW SPIFFS DATA ON WEBSITE

This project now we want to loads this state from the ESPN and when we are open the browser on the website. The website, then the spin data should be also shown on the website. So it's a usability thing. Therefore, I've created a new project file number 13 and we are opening the index Hotmail in this file.

We are adding one variable name and with the percentage sign at the beginning and the end. And this variable name we need later on in the Arduino, because then we can say, put the spivs content to this, to this variable name. So this is all we have to do in the index at the minute. Just save it. We close it and we are uploading it right now. As I told you before, I'm forgetting this point each time so that processor beyond my wife you. This is now where the next magic will happen, because now we are going at the following thing. If the variable is safe, text, this is exactly saved, not saved, and text saved a little text. This is the variable name which we are declared in the at item. If the viral variable is saved LTE text, then we can see it return. Here is some text. For example, if we do so, then in the input field will be written. Here is some text, but we want to text from the from our speed so we could call select text and referthe message, for example. But we could also use because this is in a proper description, a proper variable declaration because it's in string check, text exists. If the file exists, it returns us in string with the content. So. Return check UFOs exist, and this is all we want to do now. Safe compiler.

```cpp
44    if (!WiFi.config(local_IP, gateway, subnet, primaryDNS, secondaryDNS)) {
45      Serial.println("STA Failed to configure");
46    }
47
48    connectToAP();
49    delay(100);
50
51    server.on("/", HTTP_GET, [](AsyncWebServerRequest * request) {
52      request->send(SPIFFS, "/index.html", String(), false, processor);
53      //make a function which get the request
54                                  ) changeDisplay(checkParams(request));
55    });
56    server.on("/style.css", HTTP_GET, [](AsyncWebServerRequest * request) {
57      request->send(SPIFFS, "/style.css", "text/css");
58    });
59    server.on("/jquery.min.js", HTTP_GET, [](AsyncWebServerRequest * request) {
60      request->send(SPIFFS, "/jquery.min.js", "text/javascript");
61    });
62    server.begin();
```

And let's see what happened looks good from the compiler sites, but before we start, we have to edit a little bit here on the server because each time when you're opening the browser and type in the data, you will, then the display would be changed. That's not good because we only want to change the display when something really is changed and this could be done with requests programs that will give us back an integer, how many parents we got, we got from the server and we say if the request is greater than zero, then change my display, please, because then there should be any parameters inside. OK, now we can upload the whole sketch. The new index Atom already is already uploaded. Soothe thing is uploading the change into Cameron. OK, and now the loading text should be appear from left to right. Perfect.

```
44    if(!WiFi.config(local_IP, gateway, subnet, primaryDNS, secondaryDNS)) {
45        Serial.println("STA Failed to configure");
46    }
47
48    connectToAP();
49    delay(100);
50
51    server.on("/", HTTP_GET, [](AsyncWebServerRequest * request) {
52        request->send(SPIFFS, "/index.html", String(), false, processor);
53        //make a function which get the request
54        [                          ] changeDisplay(checkParams(request));
55    });
56    server.on("/style.css", HTTP_GET, [](AsyncWebServerRequest * request) {
57        request->send(SPIFFS, "/style.css", "text/css");
58    });
59    server.on("/jquery.min.js", HTTP_GET, [](AsyncWebServerRequest * request) {
60        request->send(SPIFFS, "/jquery.min.js", "text/javascript");
61    });
62    server.begin();
```

```
Leaving...
Hard resetting via RTS pin...
```

Then I'm opening the website. The last thing I entered was Lady, and you see, the Olympics hasn't changed until yet. Now I give out, you know, for example, show and it is perfect. Now I'm entering, yes, 32 or entering. Closing this website, opening my smartphone, for example. Refresh the page. And now the text is here is P32 now I can edit here with another device to text, speak to two six six. Will be saved and displayed on the holiday matrix. On opening once again, the. Refresh it, and with the refresh, we have also loaded to actual data. Yeah. So now we can send data from the website to the ESPN safety data to the spivs to flash memory reader flash memory. Pass the content to the website. So each site we know can send data and also get data.

CONTROL GRAPHICS AND TEXT VIA WEBSITE

Let us now edit the website in a way that we can choose the different kinds of graphics and also displayed on the leading matrix. So first of all, we go on to our new project. It's called 14 go to data and open the index file.

```
1  <!DOCTYPE html>
2  <html>
3  <head>
4      <title>LED-Matrix</title>
5      <meta name="viewport" content="width=device-width, initial-scale=1">
6      <link rel="icon" href="data:,">
7      <link rel="stylesheet" type="text/css" href="style.css">
8      <script src="jquery.min.js"></script>
9  </head>
10 <body>
11     <h2>LED-Matrix</h2>
12         <div>
13             <label for="ledtext">Text</label><br />
14             <input name="ledtext" id="ledtext" type="text" value="%safedledtext%" /><br
15
16             <fieldset class="radiobuttons">
17
18                 <label for="rocket">Rocket</label>
19                 <input type="radio" id="rocket" name="sprite">
20
21
22
23             </fieldset>
24
```

So what we can do now is we are creating here some radio buttons before the actual button comes in. Then we're closing the field set and now we are entering some label. And for example, we are going to add to the label for the rockets. And then we are seeing here and input years to type radio on. And then the idea is the same as the name. But the name of the radio button should be the same for each radio button, so that only one element could be clicked at the time. OK, so far, so good. I've created here already all the different kind of radio buttons just pasted in. For one thing, a little bit with the rocket, with type Radio I. D. Rocket Walker, you see Sprite should be each every line to sing, but type is also the same, but not the idea. Because now we want to get there with Jake where you want to get if some radio button is clicked, the text we already have. We already had. Yeah, with Jake query.

```
34          <input type="radio" id="wave" name="sprite" >
35
36          <label for="bunny">Bunny</label>
37          <input type="radio" id="bunny" name="sprite" >
38
39
40      </fieldset>
41
42          <button name="textfromled" class="button button_senden" onClick="submitGET()">show on LED Matri
43      </div>
44
45  <script>
46
47      function submitGET(){
48          var l_text = $("#ledtext").val();
49          var url="?ledtext="+l_text;
50
51
52          if($("#rocket").is(":checked")){
53              url="?rocket="+l_text;
54
55
56
57
58          console.log(url);
59
60
61
```

But now let me see. We can do that with if, for example, the LA Rockets, we're calling the idea this double point checked that we can with Chick Corea, see if some of the radio buttons are checked and then we are seeing, well, is no rocket and we are passing the text. So when someone enters and text and click on the rocket and then hits the button, this button, then the rocket should be appear as we defined it about the original and the text also will be shown. So and this could be done with that with the rest of their inputs. And as a last point, we could see this unfold pack, for example. Well, is edit text, so it's no radio button is clicked, then the usual should be deleted text with the text scrolling a little bit up. This you should be not. So, OK, now each variation should be focused. OK, check, check, check, it looks good to me, safe. And going back to his uploads this data so far so good.

```
13 }
14
15 String checkParams(AsyncWebServerRequest *request){
16    if(request->hasParam("ledtext")){
17       saveText(request->getParam("ledtext")->value());
18       return "ledtext";
19
20
21
22
23
24 }
25
26 void connectToAP() {
27    // Connect to Wi-Fi
28    WiFi.begin(ssid, password);
29    while (WiFi.status() != WL_CONNECTED) {
30       delay(1000);
31       Serial.println("Connecting to WiFi..");
```

```
Writing at 0x00290000... (33 %)
Writing at 0x00294000... (66 %)
Writing at 0x00298000... (100 %)
```

And now we have to go back to our check patterns and have to add each
line of four. Are we already included to the rocket? And also, we have to
get to know all the ifs for each of the. Graphics, therefore, I also have
created here something. Let's go through the each for each line. The
rocket to walk Pac-Man Heart Wave, Ghost Bunny, it's it. You get the clue.
It's always the same. We are refereeing from the website, the different
kind of texts and graphics with the parliament. We are saving the text to
the spoof and also returning to the string which parameter we got. And
then we can change here with this line. I'm going back with this line. We
can change the display. This is variable enough for us with the Czech
Parliament Parameters. We have fulfilled everything. So let's take a look.
So I have to change the proper function name. This is from the German
project. Now it should be done. We are not finished yet because I missed
something in the idiomatic because here scrolling a littlebit down, we
have set the text out. We know and this is not what we want. We want to
hear the message. So change. She also to a message because we want to
pass the text from the input fields. So here we go. Now we have the same
function is in the texts to attack once again. So we are changing cameras.
Those memos? Yeah, they're dark. OK, websites. Refresh the website.

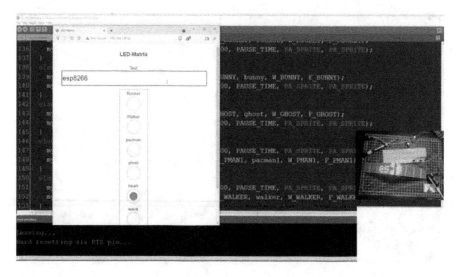

No, I'm putting in, for example, USP 32, and I want to pick men scoring a little bit down, showingany demand picks. Let's see what happens. Yes, now we're perfect too hot for USP 82 66, for example. Click on Show I. D Matrix. And now we can control the LED Matrix via the website the weight of happy interface. And if I open another window entering the website, you see the last, the last input. The text will be shown. Also here Super Super for this chapter. Now we are at the end of managing the text from the website and the get request. In the other chapter, we are dealing with some external data, for example, to reference an actualtime and cryptocurrencies to the leading matrix.

HARDWARE(ESP32 CAM) EXPLAINED

Hello again. Before getting into the project, knowing the hardware is essential one. So in this project, I'm going to get to all of these people to Kathmandu. Let's get started. What is the USB 2. 0 camera? The USB 32 camera? It's a very small camera module with a low price is P32. Yes, chip. Apart from the movie two six four zero camera, there are several job openings are available to connect with voters.

It also has a micro SD card slot that can be useful to store images taken with the camera or to store two files to solve two claims. The USB 2. 0 camera doesn't come with a USB-C connector, so you'll need an external programmer to go to school through the serial bins that you see there and transmit. It means that you have to program it. Also, we can program using audiobooks. Connections are similar to the Today program me at Amazon DSP 32 Cambodia below. What are these restrictions? I have listed all the important features of the ESB 32 camera. Let me explain one by one. The model has wireless two Wi-Fi and Bluetooth. Yes, we'll see what it is low power and capable of 32 bit processing.

Features

- The smallest 802.11b/g/n Wi-Fi BT SoC module
- Low power 32-bit CPU,can also serve the application processor
- Up to 160MHz clock speed, summary computing power up to 600 DMIPS
- Built-in 520 KB SRAM, external 4MPSRAM
- Supports UART/SPI/I2C/PWM/ADC/DAC
- Support OV2640 and OV7670 cameras, built-in flash lamp
- Support image WiFI upload
- Support TF card
- Supports multiple sleep modes
- Embedded Lwip and FreeRTOS

And it has up to 160 hertz clock speed building, in some cases 520 kilobytes. It also supports a I2C VW that EDC can and different sleep modes. It supports fully two six four zero A. V seven six seven zero cameras. That is a built-in flash alarm in this model, and it has a future of SD card slot. Instead, we can set images through Wi-Fi. Finally, this new feature of three auto is compatible. Now let's get into the keynotes of the P32 come. Let's start with the performance. This model has three bins for power source.

Pin out

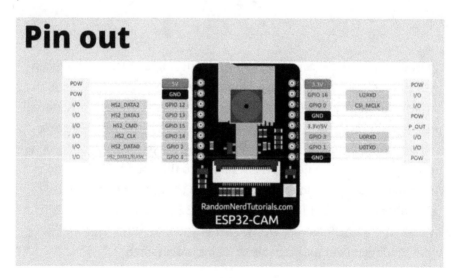

There are five old Greenwald and unknown things highlighted in red and black. Then this model has 10 GB options. They are highlighted in Purple Color GPA 01 and DPA 03 all kids who need these pins to upload the code to your world. Additionally, DPA or G2 also plays an important role since it determines whether they use Twitter to use, influencing or not. When GB zero is connected to ground the to 32 using flashing the pins highlighted by Orange is always connected with micro SD card. What are the obligations of USB 3. 0 camera module US ISP to Level six module? This all the features of that module. Apart from this, externally, this camera and micro SD card features so it can be used to that it will be need face detection or recognition, text recognition, object tracking and object detection. Using Micro SD card future, we can save the images and projects taken while project training. Let's take a look at the project in this project. The interface motion sensor whenever motion detects it, takes images and stores like this. We can use instead of USB 2. 0 six module, but the only problem is lack of mini GPUs. Eastland, I covered all the necessary details of SB 32, Cameron wanted. Let's see in next project. Thank you.

EXPLANATION OF ARDUINO SOFTWARE

Hello, friends. Welcome back. In previous projects, we are seen onboard hardware used in this project, and it's coming since now we are entering into software. It's to through this project, it's working in this project. We are going to use audio software for programming the USB 32 camera module. Let's discuss about this after. Here is the software to download this go to or in order to see that I'm going to download Beach according to your operating system you can download. It is an easy step to do, then install after installation. Open it. It looks like this. Top of the software consist of file name and version that you downloaded, and below this you can see five functions. Those are file you did sketch tools and helper using file function.

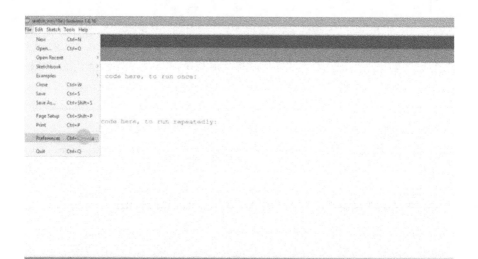

We can do save open Brent could the files, and we can take some example programs, according to the vote preferences contained settings of this software.

SETUP FOR ESP32 CAM IN ARDUINO

I'm going to give some instructions to set up the boats and labelling requirements for SB 32 can. It's being forced to step open fire, elemental unclear preferences and the inferences you can see attitude towards manager your option in this you should based SB 32. Campbell, you are.

This is for access. More details by ordinance of the. Next to step is to install East P32 Ward in the softer selected tools, mainly in this clipboards and ward manager.

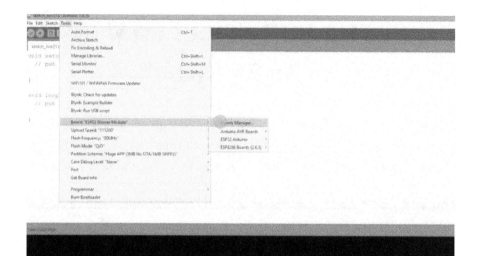

It will take some time to pop up new window in this type SB 32 in search where. You can see ESB 32 ward in library. Then click Install.

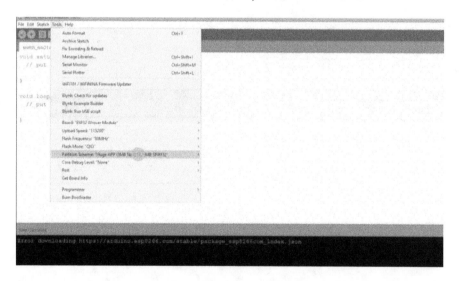

Third and final step open tools mean select board and click Ease P32 or email, and then select the ESB 32 role model, then Lethem's your uploading speed is low 150 200 and then flat frequency is 18minutes. I'm next plus mode is ku a and partisan scheme should be huge. And that's it. Finally, and more importantly, port selection also ensure you selected the correct port. That said, I covered all the necessary steps to set up the environment. Please do us the. Thank you.

What is ?

What is the FDA monitor the FDA used to deal silicone converter module, is it universal synchronously receiver transmitted to use the word digital seal communication? It is popularly used to for communication to and from microcontroller development goals such as ESP zero one and all new macros, which do not have USB interfaces.

Pin out

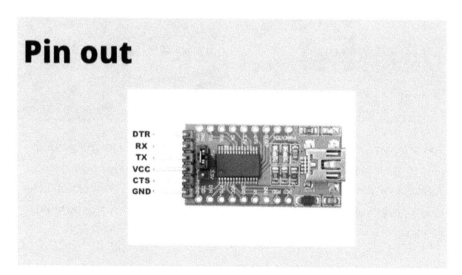

Let's discuss the Pagination connections. This model has six pins. Apart from this, the more commonly used to pin 30x onyx green and green pins,

131

these pins should be connected to respective pins of SPF 32 Campbell. We only used this model for programming these P32 money. That's why I'm not going to take a feeding module in full detail.

CONNECTION WITH ARDUINO UNO

If. Very good to see you again in this project, we can program the SB 32 cam deal with our remote lake audio, you know, na no unacceptable. I will show you how to program the USB 32 cam model with, you know what? Let's jump into the connection, connect you to two days of training and connect ESB 32 cams.

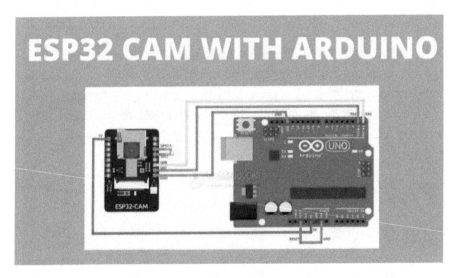

You are two orix of the arena and then connect via voltage and ground pins to their respective pins, then showed the ordinary zip in the ground. Finally, saw the a huge after enough speak to probe this connection is for to get programming mode in iOS P32. OK. That's all about programming connections with our Let's See next project.

LIVE STREAM CODING AND EXPLANATIONS

I'm going to explain the GOAT to get this code go to fight and make symbols in the examples, go to your speed 32, then click Camera.

Finally, click Air Speed 32, the camera now full files opened in ordinance after it in those files. First warning named sweep. So it is executable a no fight and second one named as it is for the functions while project streaming on the observer. Next, there will be camera index and camera pin files for the camera information's. First, let me explain camera to fight in this file, which includes two USB P32 camera on camera, things, hidden face and widely labelled device. Then, according to the board manufacture, we should select the mode for myself. 18 cérémonie next. My favorite Ince's in this enter your asystole and password of your network, then some line of code for defining camera.

```
CameraWebServer | Arduino 1.8.16
File  Edit  Sketch  Tools  Help

CameraWebServer §
  if (s->id.PID == OV3660_PID) {
    s->set_vflip(s, 1); // flip it back
    s->set_brightness(s, 1); // up the brightness just a bit
    s->set_saturation(s, -2); // lower the saturation
  }

  // drop down frame size for higher initial frame rate
  s->set_framesize(s, FRAMESIZE_QVGA);

#if defined(CAMERA_MODEL_M5STACK_WIDE) || defined(CAMERA_MODEL_M5STACK_ESP32CAM)
  s->set_vflip(s, 1);
  s->set_hmirror(s, 1);
#endif

  WiFi.begin(ssid, password);

  while (WiFi.status() != WL_CONNECTED) {
    delay(500);
    Serial.print(".");
  }
  Serial.println("");
  Serial.println("WiFi connected");

  startCameraServer();
}
```

```
Sketch uses 2594774 bytes (82%) of program storage space. Maximum is 3145728 bytes.
Global variables use 56256 bytes (17%) of dynamic memory, leaving 271424 bytes for local variables. Maximum is 327680 bytes.
```

Finally, some line of code for WiFi connections. Next to fail is up a steep fight. It is C++ fighting for the functions that is stored steam gained steam and extra wine. VIDEO Running on the web server dysfunction God placed in great corners for this file is used next to two files our camera index and camera pins. These are the two header files for defining camera, and it's been. Let's applaud the code in two years, Peter Little Kamhawi first to FTD or already know that SB 32 can more than open tools menu, then select the USB 32 role model and uploading speed is less than 50 200and then flash frequencies 80 might then flash Montesquieu, Ivo and portals and scheme should be huge app finally, and importantly, select respective port that DSP digital camera connected. Next step is to uploading to the vote, to upload click upload button. First, it will come by local. Wait, it takes some time to get uploaded after upload that you can see then uploading. While applauding, you need to click the Eastern button for to get in. Good morning, East, Peter, you can after upload it, remove the DPA zero two ground connection in East P32 can then click the Restart button. Now open, this really wanted to instill monitor, you can see why you connected a message.

And it's also the IP address that is assigned to USP. Copy that IP address and paste it in the of to see the result.

LIVE VIDEO STREAMING DEMO ON ESP32 CAM

Open your browser and based on the IP address that is copied from the serial monitor after loading. You can see camera running in the observer right corner. You can see several camera functions.

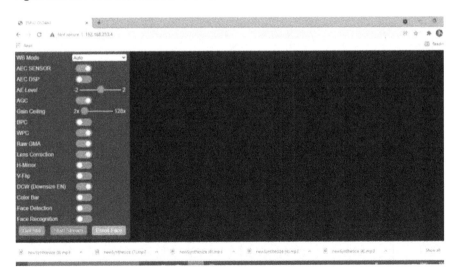

If you want to take these functions, go on and check. OK, friends, I explained how to make life video streaming on local IP address and some steps to do go on, make it yourself. The goal is in

ESP32 CAM - CODE EXPLAINED

Every six, including Gusau in the U. S. , so go into that section and feel free to copy the codes from it. Let's discuss the code. First, we enclosed to web and why claimed library files? Also, I declared War on Swords Fight. In this, we declared the camera in Nick's file and also I have enclosed camera pins header fight. Then we need to select more, according to the manufacturer, we should select next.

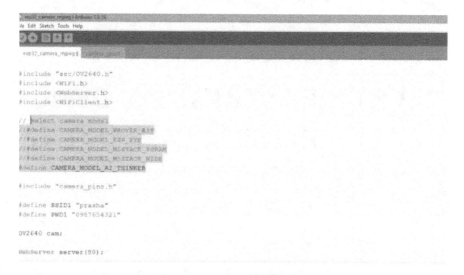

```
#include "src/OV2640.h"
#include <WiFi.h>
#include <WebServer.h>
#include <WiFiClient.h>

// select camera model
//#define CAMERA_MODEL_WROVER_KIT
//#define CAMERA_MODEL_ESP_EYE
//#define CAMERA_MODEL_M5STACK_PSRAM
//#define CAMERA_MODEL_M5STACK_WIDE
#define CAMERA_MODEL_AI_THINKER

#include "camera_pins.h"

#define SSID1 "prasha"
#define PWD1 "0987654321"

OV2640 cam;

WebServer server(80);
```

Why do you think entails such as a society and password of your network? Then some line of code for accessing the observer server, then another some lines describes ghamro connections. Finally, some lines for why you think credentials. If one is connected, it prints why he is connected in serial monitor. Is it prints disconnected in the camera or pins header file? They are only been connections of the camera for this after understanding purpose.

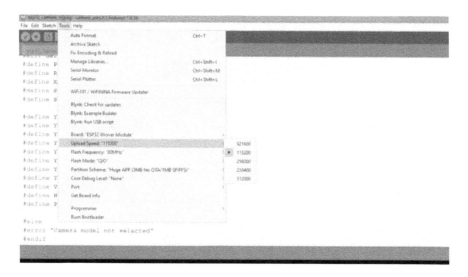

Let's set up the required tools as following open tools and select mood as you speak, 32 Rover Money been uploading speeds 150 200 then plus frequencies 80 had been mode is huge, a mixed and schemes should be huge. Finally, and importantly, Port, which is ESP 32, is connected. OK, now we discussed about the quote unquote set ups. Let's upload the code. Let's combine the code. Please remember while uploading, we need to be stored within and after upload. We need to remove ground to use zero connection in these P32 can finally press upload button.

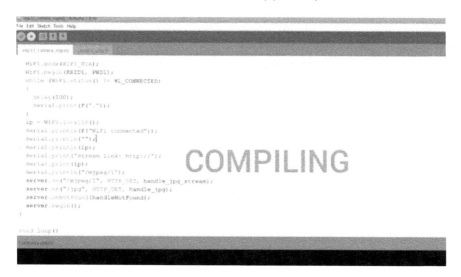

Please ensure would set up certain.

BLYNK APP SETUP FOR VIDEO STREAMING

we are going to set up the link application for live video streaming. Let's get started. First, install an open link application, then create a new project.

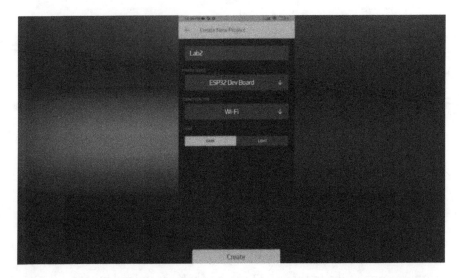

In this, you need to give project name, give any name you want, then select these P32 development will then prescreened you choose all to organize into your email. The new name on token for this project, you're going to make this project using local IP address, so only then press play second and select video streaming it. Finally, click on the widget and face to the various streaming app. Now the app is set for the project.

FACE AND EYE RECOGNITION PROJECT EXPLAINED

Hello again. You may wonder how face detection and recognition is possible using a speaker to Cambodia. Yes, it is possible through Python programming. Hope you can help us. We know Python has inbuilt libraries for open TV.

This open TV has a library for a related operations like this AI based recognition and makes it using this open TV library. Python language recognizes the faces. OK, now we know how the face recognition works. Let's discuss how we speak to look and works in face and eye recognition. First is Peter Cameron's normally livestreaming program. Then it will run livestreaming using local IP. Invite them. We ran this race and I think it needs some Python libraries in Python code. Let's discuss the code.

FACE AND EYE RECOGNITION – CODE

Hello again, this section calling is divided into two, those are, you know, and by then programming in audio programming, it's nothing just like wife livestreaming program. Let's see this first.

I enclosed some required libraries, then wife credentials, and next some setting codes for camera resolution and some line of codes to control streaming related operations. That's it. Let's upload the code into your speed. The little camera first to connect FTD or Reno with the USB 2. 0 camera and then open tools and then select the ECB.

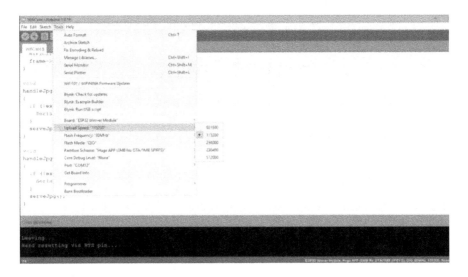

The Little Rover Module and uploading speed is 150 200. And then flash frequency is 80 marked. Then flash mode is huge and partisan scheme should be huge up. Finally, and importantly, you select respective put that DSP the little camera connected. Take some time to get uploaded after uploaded open serial monitor and crispy start button once after, you can see local IP. Copy that? It will be useful in programming.

141

INSTALLING PYTHON SOFTWARE

We will see how do install Python software and how to install required libraries using command prompt? Let's begin. It is easy to install Python on your machine. First, open your browser and search for it and download. Then click First Search Result.

It will redirect you into download page.

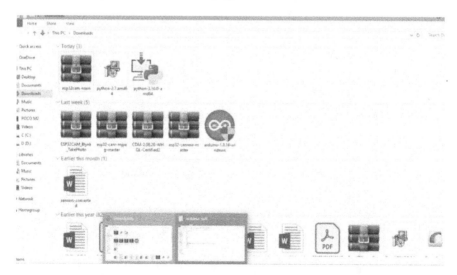

Then, according to your machine, you can download after downloaded double click on the execute fight. It is very easy to do. It will ask for permission, then automatically it will be installed for myself already installed.

INSTALLING REQUIRED PYTHON LIBRARIES IN COMMAND PROMPT(CMD)

After avoidance of duty installed, we need to install required libraries in command prompt, so open the command prompt and enter will be installed no before no library and enter before install open TV Python for next to library.

That's it. We then the required steps for running Python code.

FACE AND EYE RECOGNITION PROJECT – DEMO

https://sanet.st/blogs/bonnytuts/

Open by themselves to then copy the code from Resource six and explaining this Python code takes too much time. Simply, this cauldrons open civil libraries for face and eye recognition in local IP network.

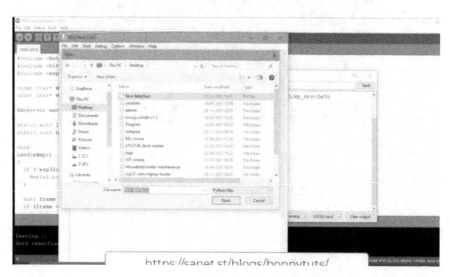

https://sanet.st/blogs/bonnytuts/

The only change we need to do is based local IP addresses in Python code.

After the changes first run module, it will run low transmission using local IP network. You can see if it's an isolated thing. That's it. We've done this project. Do it yourself.

EXPLANATION ABOUT MAILCLIENT LIBRARY AND INSTALLATION

Welcome in the studio video, I will explain how the email playing library works and how to install it into our new software to send emails with the ESRB 32 cam. We will use the USB 32 million lane library. This library allows the USB 32 cam to send and receive emails with or without attachment via some deep and iimi B servers. And this project will use your SMTP to send an email with an attachment. The attachment isa a photo taken with these Peter loo can simply be mean simple mail transfer protocol and Edison Internet Standard for email transmission. To send e-mail through the code, you need to know your ID simply be sold. It details because A. T. M. Royden has a different SPV, so now we will see about how to install play library in our software. For this opens gets me no.

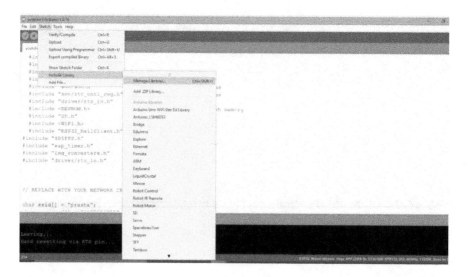

And click on Include Library in this click on Manage Library. It takes some time to pop up new window.

PROJECT CODE – EXPLANATION

Let me explain the code for this project. This written code is in the U. S. Feel free to copy this. This code takes a photo in the East 32 camp festivals and sends it to your email account before uploading the code. Make sure you insert you send that e-mail clippings as well as your recipient e-mail first input to record libraries. These P32 mail shortage is used to send emails. The first audit on the switch started to audit user to access and save files.

Disputes under the way Feed Audit Library used useful to utilize wifely and connect to your USB 32 county, your local network and insert your network credentials in the following the words then 90 minutes in miracle on the humans and the country able and its password on in image and work was already in the next line of code into the recipient's email. This is the email that will receive the email sent by ESB 32, then insert your e-mail provider SMTP settings on the following links We are using the settings for its email account. If you are using a different naming provider replace with the corresponding SMB settings, then we need to create subject of the image. The end of the email subject on the email subject variable, then create an SMTP data object called some DB data that contains the data to send through email and all other configurations. Next, some line of code defines the camera pins and some line of code for spoofs mounting next to the space, noting some lines experience about the camera initialization. After this, this code is useful to take picture with ease with can look be the mistakenly installed as site in JPG format and afterwards its in photo by email to the recipient image provided before after send. It will print image successfully. Send on the scene and monitor that system or code. Let me upload the code.

After the gold is uploaded, open city monitored and reset button now it's also an interconnected spoofs mounted on finally source image since successfully the images sent by eagles to be 32 years sewn on demo video.

BLYNK APPLICATION SETUP

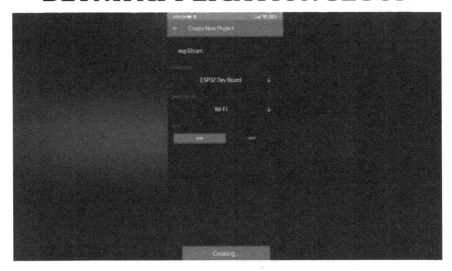

Next, blink applications settle for this project, first install and open the application, then click New Project. First, we need to give name of the product, then select Devices Speed 32 development. But after this, click create. It's also our token for this project to ease into your email, lady. So go and coffee that it is needed in our code.

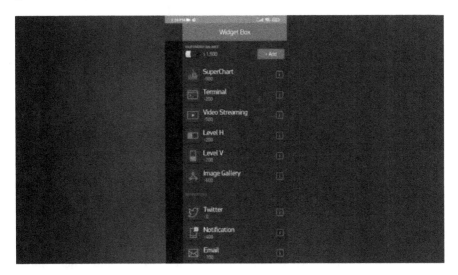

Then click on Plus button and select the image gallery. Then it and we need to create one button and then go and select one button if you click on this widget. It's all some settings in been. Select Jill 14:40 Musicality and four for.

CODE EXPLANATIONS FOR PROJECT 6

First, we will discuss about the. This audio file continues to four ways. Those are shown here. Apart from these files is Peter O'Toole Blink Take photo file its main fight. Other files are supporting files. These supporting files consist camera settings, and it's been declaration. Let's discuss the code in Maine faith. First and foremost, thing we need to do is including requiring libraries for this project like wife and bling related libraries. We no need to install new library for this project because already we did one project using Link Deplat for min next line. We declare to the world, according to the manufacturer, and next we include the camera up in headed fight. Next, we define blink our footprints for camera and if it is easier to turn on or off the camera.

On next to some lines, we declared a in credentials such as society and Bossert and Link token. Next, we declare some variables and functions. Take photo function is used to capture the images invited to function. We declare about the gamut of things and based on the things BSM is used to for higher resolution. Next, some lines disclaimers about the camera initialization and some indication to report in Seattle, Washington. Finally, why no function continuously since captured images to blink application. Patients who are the world's settings are correctly chosen. That system only called.

TELEGRAM APP SETUP FOR THE PROJECT

First, we are going to set up little grandma for this project. Let's get started. Open Telegram and search for bot for the in search box. Then clicking this, then click start. Then send new word come in, then it asks for a name given name.

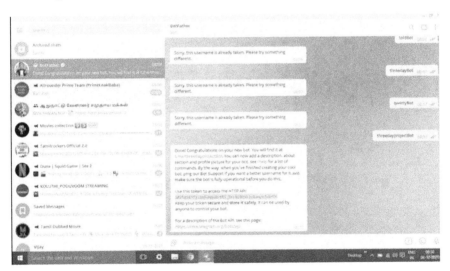

Again, it asks for you, suddenly enter it. Now you received a token for your username. It is useful in. After this search for a reward, then open it and click start. Vincent's last get 80 command. It will send your Telegram 80 copied and pasted in our code.

INSTALLING REQUIRED TELEGRAM LIBRARIES

We tend to look at them setups. Now we are going to install some required libraries. We need R. E. M. , Jason and Universal KG for libraries for this open Scotsman and click Include library, then manage libraries. It will pop up new window in this search for orientation.

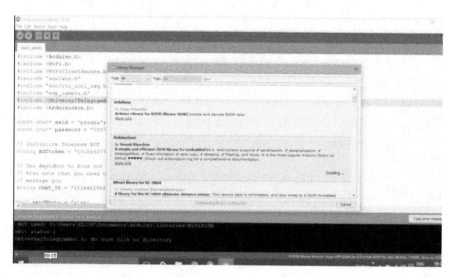

Then click Install the correct library.

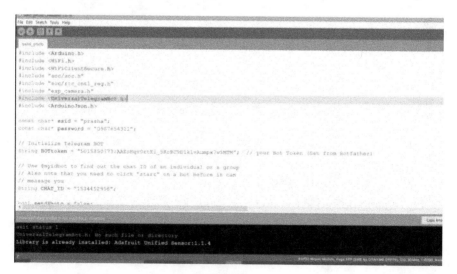

Now we need Universal Telegram bot label to download this open browser and search this name and click GitHub Link, then download as like. To include this again, go to statesman and click Include Library then and Replay will have to select the file downloaded before. Now being lost, all the good libraries that sit.

PROJECT CODE – EXPLAINED

First and foremost, the thing we need to do is including libraries for this project, like wifely and Telegram related rate relief on next to some lines. We declare the wife credentials, such as ethnicity and password and telegram of token.

Next, we declare the variables falls in four photo and lastly, this line of code takes for a new request every second. Then we declare a multi-camera pins and on two things, the Ethereum user for higher resolution. Next, some lines described above the camera initialization and next and a new message function deals with a request sent from the Telegram model seen for Telegram function deals with image sending to Telegram invited to function.

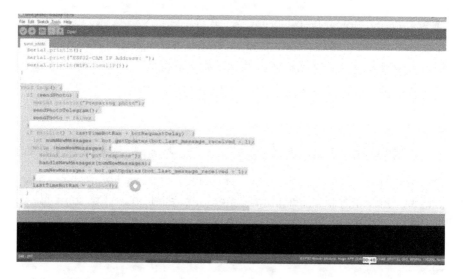

We declare no Flashlight NYC later this responses. Finally, this this look continuously send captured images to KG. Please ensure the water settings automatically chosen that suitable to code its upload.

SERIAL MONITOR RESULT

After uploaded opens, we'll monitor it all the way through connected and Telegram may be connected.

If we send photo command, it sent images to Telegram.

DEMO - SENDING CAPTURED IMAGES TO TELEGRAM

I'm going to show output in kilogram up the user username in Telegram app. He will open a new tactic. And in this click start Vincent's last photo comment to receive photo and flash floods command for flashinglight to turn our flashlight.

You'll need to send flash command again. Here you can see the images captured using USB 32 Campbell. Here are some photos taken using news people who can let's see one by one. 38 guys. See you soon.

www.ingramcontent.com/pod-product-compliance
Lightning Source LLC
LaVergne TN
LVHW022124060326
832903LV00063B/3696